Overpopulation is now the dominant problem in all our personal, national, and international planning.

No one can do rational personal planning, nor can public policy be resolved in any area, unless one first takes into account the population bomb.

Schools, politicians, and mass media only touch the edge of the major problem.

Dr. Paul R. Ehrlich is Bing Professor of Population Studies at Stanford University. His specialty is population biology. He has written over one hundred scientific papers and more than a dozen books on this and related subjects.

Also by Paul R. Ehrlich
Published by Ballantine Books:

THE END OF AFFLUENCE (*with Anne H. Ehrlich*)

EXTINCTION: The Causes and Consequences of the
Disappearance of Species (*with Anne H. Ehrlich*)

THE
POPULATION
BOMB
(Revised)

Dr. Paul R. Ehrlich

BALLANTINE BOOKS • NEW YORK

ISBN 0-345-33834-0

Printed in Canada

First Edition: May 1968

Revised Edition:
First Printing: February 1971
Twentieth Printing: December 1989

To Lisa

CONTENTS

CONTENTS

THE
POPULATION
BOMB

PROLOGUE

The battle to feed all of humanity is over. In the 1970s and 1980s hundreds of millions of people will starve to death in spite of any crash programs embarked upon now. At this late date nothing can prevent a substantial increase in the world death rate, although many lives could be saved through dramatic programs to "stretch" the carrying capacity of the earth by increasing food production and providing for more equitable distribution of whatever food is available. But these programs will only provide a stay of execution unless they are accompanied by determined and successful efforts at population control. Population control is the conscious regulation of the numbers of human beings to meet the needs not just of individual families, but of society as a whole.

Nothing could be more misleading to our children than our present affluent society. They will inherit a totally different world, a world in which the standards, politics, and economics of the past decade are dead. As the most influential nation in the world today, and its largest consumer, the United States cannot stand isolated. We are today involved in the events leading to famine and ecocatastrophe; tomorrow we may be destroyed by them.

Our position requires that we take immediate action at home and promote effective action worldwide. We must have population control at home, hopefully through changes in our value system, but by compulsion if voluntary methods fail. Americans must also change their way of living so as to minimize their impact on the world's resources and environment. Programs which combine ecologically sound agricultural development and population control must be established and supported in underdeveloped countries. While this is being done, we must take action to reverse the deterioration of our environment before our planet is permanently ruined. It cannot be overemphasized, however, that no changes in behavior or technology can save us unless we can achieve control over the size of the human population. The birth rate must be brought into balance with the death rate or mankind will breed itself into oblivion. We can no longer afford merely to treat the symptoms of the cancer of population growth; the cancer itself must be cut out.

FOREWORD

Man can undo himself with no other force than his own brutality. It is a new brutality, coming swiftly at a time when, as Loren Eiseley says, "the need is for a gentler race. But the hand that hefted the axe against the ice, the tiger, and the bear now fondles the machine gun as lovingly."

The roots of the new brutality, it will become clear from *The Population Bomb,* are in the lack of population control. There is, we must hope and predict, a chance to exert control in time. We would like to predict that organizations which, like the Sierra Club, have been much too calm about the ultimate threat to mankind, will awaken themselves and others, and awaken them with an urgency that will be necessary to fulfillment of the prediction that mankind will survive.

It was only twelve years ago that we even suggested, in any Sierra Club publication, that uncontrolled population was a menace. We went far enough to write: "People are recognizing that we cannot forever continue to multiply and subdue the earth without losing our standard of life and the natural beauty that must be part of it. . . . These are the years of decision—the decision of men to stay the flood of man."

In the next two years we worried about the battle of man versus his own numbers and were concerned that growth itself was growing and were not joyful about the imminence of California's outstripping New York.

It was Professor Raymond Cowles who shook us loose with a provocative address before a Sierra Club conference, "The Meaning of Wilderness to Science."

What in the late fifties had seemed heretical soon was not so. For the complaints that I had received about mentioning population problems in early speeches, there were more vociferous complaints if I forgot to mention the big problem. In just two or three years it became possible to question growth, to suggest that DNA was greater than GNP, to predict that man had enough genius to require that science and technology be put to good purpose. He could limit his numbers. He could limit his heretofore unslackened appetite for destroying wilderness. He could go back over the nine-tenths or so of the earth that had already felt his touch, sometimes a gentle touch but too often brutal, and do better where he had been. He could start with Manhattan, or Los Angeles.

Whatever resources the wilderness still held would not sustain him in his old habits of growing and reaching without limits. Wilderness could, however, provide answers for questions he had not yet learned how to ask. He could predict that the day of creation was not over, that there would be wiser men, and they would thank him for leaving the source of those answers. Wilderness would remain part of his geography of hope, as Wallace Stegner put it, and could, merely because wilderness endured on the planet, prevent man's world from becoming a cage.

The good predictions could be entertained—the notion of predicting a more and more desirable future, not just a more and more crowded one.

—DAVID BROWER

Chapter 1
THE PROBLEM

I have understood the population explosion intellectually for a long time. I came to understand it emotionally one stinking hot night in Delhi a few years ago. My wife and daughter and I were returning to our hotel in an ancient taxi. The seats were hopping with fleas. The only functional gear was third. As we crawled through the city, we entered a crowded slum area. The temperature was well over 100, and the air was a haze of dust and smoke. The streets seemed alive with people. People eating, people washing, people sleeping. People visiting, arguing, and screaming. People thrusting their hands through the taxi window, begging. People defecating and urinating. People clinging to buses. People herding animals. People, people, people, people. As we moved slowly through the mob, hand horn squawking, the dust, noise, heat, and cooking fires gave the scene a hellish aspect. Would we ever get to our hotel? All three of us were, frankly, frightened. It seemed that anything could happen—but, of course, nothing did. Old India hands will laugh at our reaction. We were just some overprivileged tourists, unaccustomed to the sights and sounds of India. Perhaps, but the problems of Delhi and Calcutta are our problems too. Americans have helped to create them; we help to prevent their solution. We must all learn to identify with the plight of our less fortunate fellows on Spaceship Earth if we are to help both them and ourselves to survive.

Too Many People

Americans are beginning to realize that the under-developed countries of the world face an inevitable population-food crisis. Each year food production in these countries falls a bit further behind burgeoning population growth, and people go to bed a little bit hungrier. While there are temporary or local reversals of this trend, it now seems inevitable that it will continue to its logical conclusion: mass starvation. The rich may continue to get richer, but the more numerous poor are going to get poorer. Of these poor, a *minimum* of ten million people, most of them children, will starve to death during each year of the 1970s. But this is a mere handful compared to the numbers that will be starving before the end of the century. And it is now too late to take action to save many of those people.

However, most Americans are not aware that the U.S. and other developed countries also have a problem with overpopulation. Rather than suffering from food short-ages, these countries show symptoms in the form of environmental deterioration and increased difficulty in obtaining resources to support their affluence.

In a book about population there is a temptation to stun the reader with an avalanche of statistics. I'll spare you most, but not all, of that. After all, no matter how you slice it, population is a numbers game. Perhaps the

3

best way to impress you with numbers is to tell you about the "doubling time"—the time necessary for the population to double in size.

It has been estimated that the human population of 8000 B.C. was about five million people, taking perhaps one million years to get there from two and a half million. The population did not reach 500 million until almost 10,000 years later—about 1650 A.D. This means it doubled roughly once every thousand years or so. It reached a billion people around 1850, doubling in some 200 years. It took only 80 years or so for the next doubling, as the population reached two billion around 1930. We have not completed the next doubling to four billion yet, but we now have well over three and a half billion people. The doubling time at present seems to be about 35 years.[1] Quite a reduction in doubling times: 1,000,000 years, 1,000 years, 200 years, 80 years, 35 years. Perhaps the meaning of a doubling time of around 35 years is best brought home by a theoretical exercise. Let's examine what might happen on the absurd assumption that the population continued to double every 35 years into the indefinite future.

If growth continued at that rate for about 900 years, there would be some 60,000,000,000,000,000 people on the face of the earth. Sixty million billion people. This is about 100 persons for each square yard of the Earth's surface, land and sea. A British physicist, J. H. Fremlin,[2] guessed that such a multitude might be housed in a continuous 2,000-story building covering our entire planet. The upper 1,000 stories would contain only the apparatus for running this gigantic warren. Ducts, pipes, wires, elevator shafts, etc., would occupy about half of the space in the bottom 1,000 stories. This would leave three or four yards of floor space for each person. I will leave to your imagination the physical details of existence in this ant heap, except to point out that all would not be black. Probably each person would be limited in his travel. Perhaps he could take elevators through all 1,000 residential stories but could travel only within a circle of a few hundred yards' radius on any floor. This would permit, however, each person to choose his friends from among some ten million people! And, as Fremlin points out, entertainment on the worldwide TV should be excellent, for at any time "one could expect some ten million Shakespeares and rather more Beatles to be alive."

Could growth of the human population of the Earth continue beyond that point? Not according to Fremlin. We would have reached a "heat limit." People themselves, as well as their activities, convert other forms of energy into heat which must be dissipated. In order to permit this excess heat to radiate directly from the top of the "world building" directly into space, the atmosphere would have been pumped into flasks under the sea well before the limiting population size was reached. The precise limit would depend on the technology of the day. At a population size of one billion billion people, the temperature of the "world roof" would be kept around the melting point of iron to radiate away the human heat generated.

But, you say, surely Science (with a capital "S") will find a way for us to occupy the other planets of our solar system and eventually of other stars before we get all that crowded. Skip for a moment the virtual certainty that those planets are uninhabitable. Forget also the insurmountable logistic problems of moving billions of people off the Earth. Fremlin has made some interesting calculations on how much time we could buy by occupying the planets of the solar system. For instance, at any given time it would take only about 50 years to populate Venus, Mercury, Mars, the moon, and the moons of Jupiter and Saturn to the same population density as Earth.[3]

What if the fantastic problems of reaching and colo-

nizing the other planets of the solar system, such as
Jupiter and Uranus, can be solved? It would take only
about 200 years to fill them "Earth-full." So we could
perhaps gain 250 years of time for population growth in
the solar system after we had reached an absolute limit
on Earth. What then? We can't ship our surplus to the
stars. Professor Garrett Hardin[4] of the University of
California at Santa Barbara has dealt effectively with
this fantasy. Using extremely optimistic assumptions, he
has calculated that Americans, by cutting their standard
of living down to 18% of its present level, could in *one
year* set aside enough capital to finance the exportation
to the stars of *one day's* increase in the population of
the world.

Interstellar transport for surplus people presents an
amusing prospect. Since the ships would take generations
to reach most stars, the only people who could be trans-
ported would be those willing to exercise strict birth
control. Population explosions on space ships would be
disastrous. Thus we would have to export our responsible people, leaving the irresponsible at home on Earth
to breed.

Enough of fantasy. Hopefully, you are convinced that
the population will have to stop growing sooner or later
and that the extremely remote possibility of expanding
into outer space offers no escape from the laws of population growth. If you still want to hope for the stars, just
remember that, at the current growth rate, in a few
thousand years everything in the visible universe would
be converted into people, and the ball of people would
be expanding with the speed of light![5] Unfortunately,
even 900 years is much too far in the future for those
of us concerned with the population explosion. As you
will see, the next *nine* years will probably tell the story.

Of course, population growth is not occurring uniformly over the face of the Earth. Indeed, countries
are divided rather neatly into two groups: those with

rapid growth rates, and those with relatively slow growth rates. The first group, making up about two-thirds of the world population, coincides closely with what are known as the "underdeveloped countries" (UDCs). The UDCs are not industrialized, tend to have inefficient agriculture, very small gross national products, high illiteracy rates and related problems. That's what UDCs are technically, but a short definition of underdeveloped is "hungry." Most Latin American, African, and Asian countries fall into this category. The second group consists of the "overdeveloped countries" (ODCs). ODCs are modern industrial nations, such as the United States, Canada, most European countries, Israel, the USSR, Japan, and Australia. They consume a disproportionate amount of the world's resources and are the major polluters. Most, but by no means all,[6] people in these countries are adequately nourished.

Doubling times in the UDCs range around 20 to 35 years. Examples of these times (from the 1970 figures released by the Population Reference Bureau) are: Kenya, 23 years; Nigeria, 27; Turkey, 26; Indonesia, 24; Philippines, 21; Brazil, 25; Costa Rica, 19; and El Salvador, 21. Think of what it means for the population of a country to double in 25 years. In order just to keep living standards at the present inadequate level, the food available for the people must be doubled. Every structure and road must be duplicated. The amount of power must be doubled. The capacity of the transport system must be doubled. The number of trained doctors, nurses, teachers, and administrators must be doubled. This would be a fantastically difficult job in the United States—a rich country with a fine agricultural system, immense industries, and access to abundant resources. Think of what it means to a country with none of these.

Remember also that in virtually all UDCs, people have gotten the word about the better life it is possible to have. They have seen colored pictures in magazines of the miracles of Western technology. They have seen automobiles and airplanes. They have seen American and European movies. Many have seen refrigerators, tractors, and even TV sets. Almost all have heard transistor radios. They *know* that a better life is possible. They have what we like to call "rising expectations." If twice as many people are to be happy, the miracle of doubling what they now have will not be enough. It will only maintain today's standard of living. There will have to be a tripling or better. Needless to say, they are not going to be happy.

Doubling times for the populations of the ODCs tend to be in the 50-to-200-year range. Examples of 1970 doubling times are the United States, 70 years; Austria, 175; Denmark, 88; Norway, 78; United Kingdom, 140; Poland, 78; Russia, 70; Italy, 88; Spain, 70; and Japan, 63. These are industrialized countries that have undergone the so-called demographic transition—a transition from high to low growth rates. As industrialization progressed, children became less important to parents as extra hands to work on the farm and as support in old age. At the same time they became a financial drag —expensive to raise and educate. Presumably these were the reasons for a slowing of population growth after industrialization. They boil down to a simple fact —people just wanted to have fewer children.

It is important to emphasize, however, that the demographic transition does not result in zero population growth, but in a growth rate which in many of the most important ODCs results in populations doubling every seventy years or so. This means, for instance, that even if most UDCs were to undergo a demographic transition (of which there is no sign) the world would still be faced by catastrophic population growth. *No growth rate can be sustained in the long run.*

Saying that the ODCs have undergone a demographic transition thus does not mean that they have no population problems. First of all, most of them are already overpopulated. They are overpopulated by the simple criterion that they are not able to produce enough food to feed their populations. It is true that they have the money to buy food, but when food is no longer available for sale they will find the money rather indigestible. Similarly, ODCs are overpopulated because they do not themselves have the resources to support their affluent societies; they must coopt much more than their fair share of the world's wealth of minerals and energy. And they are overpopulated because they have exceeded the capacity of their environments to dispose of their wastes. Remember, overpopulation does not normally mean too many people for the area of a country, but too many people in relation to the necessities and amenities of life. *Overpopulation occurs when numbers threaten values.*

ODCs also share with the UDCs serious problems of population distribution. Their urban centers are getting more and more crowded relative to the countryside. This problem is not as severe in ODCs as it is in the UDCs (if current trends should continue, which they cannot, Calcutta would have 66 million inhabitants in the year 2000), but they are very serious and speedily worsening. In the United States, one of the more rapidly growing ODCs, we hear constantly of the headaches related to growing cities: not just garbage in our environment, but overcrowded highways, burgeoning slums, deteriorating school systems, rising tax and crime rates, riots, and other social disorders. Indeed, social and environmental problems not only increase with growing population and urbanization, they tend to increase at an even faster rate. Adding more people to an area increases the damage done by each individual. Doubling the population normally much more than doubles environmental deterioration.[7]

Demographically, the whole problem is quite simple. A population will continue to grow as long as the birth rate exceeds the death rate—if immigration and emigration are not occurring. It is, of course, the balance between birth rate and death rate that is critical. The birth rate is the number of births per thousand people per year in the population. The death rate is the number of deaths per thousand people per year.[8] Subtracting the death rate from the birth rate, ignoring migration, gives the rate of increase. If the birth rate is 30 per thousand per year, and the death rate is 10 per thousand per year, then the rate of increase is 20 per thousand per year $(30 - 10 = 20)$. Expressed as a percent (rate per hundred people), the rate of 20 per thousand becomes 2%. If the rate of increase is 2%, then the doubling time will be 35 years. Note that if you simply added 20 people per thousand per year to the population, it would take 50 years to add a second thousand people ($20 \times 50 = 1,000$). But the doubling time is actually much less because populations grow at compound interest rates. Just as interest dollars themselves earn interest, so people added to population produce more people. It's growing at compound interest that makes populations double so much more rapidly than seems possible. Look at the relationship between the annual percent increase (interest rate) and the doubling time of the population (time for your money to double):

Annual percent increase	Doubling time
1.0	70
2.0	35
3.0	24
4.0	17

Those are all the calculations—I promise. If you are interested in more details on how demographic figuring is done, you may enjoy reading Thompson and Lewis's excellent book, *Population Problems*,[9] or my book, *Population, Resources, Environment*. [10]

There are some professional optimists around who like to greet every sign of dropping birth rates with wild pronouncements about the end of the population explosion. They are a little like a person who, after a low temperature of five below zero on December 21, interprets a low of only three below zero on December 22 as a cheery sign of approaching spring. First of all, birth rates, along with all demographic statistics, show short-term fluctuations caused by many factors. For instance, the birth rate depends rather heavily on the number of women at reproductive age. In the United States the low birth rates of the late 1960's are being replaced by higher rates as more post World War II "baby boom" children move into their reproductive years. In Japan, 1966, the Year of the Fire Horse, was a year of very low birth rates. There is widespread belief that girls born in the Year of the Fire Horse make poor wives, and Japanese couples try to avoid giving birth in that year because they are afraid of having daughters.

But, I repeat, it is the relationship between birth rate and death rate that is most critical. Indonesia, Laos, and Haiti all had birth rates around 46 per thousand in 1966. Costa Rica's birth rate was 41 per thousand. Good for Costa Rica? Unfortunately, not very. Costa Rica's death rate was less than nine per thousand, while the other countries all had death rates above 20 per thousand. The population of Costa Rica in 1966 was doubling every 17 years, while the doubling times of Indonesia, Laos, and Haiti were all above 30 years. Ah, but, you say, it was good for Costa Rica—fewer people per thousand were dying each year. Fine for a few years perhaps, but what then? Some 50% of the people in Costa Rica are under 15 years old. As they get older, they will need more and more food in a world with less and less. In 1983 they will have twice as many mouths to feed as they had in 1966, if the 1966 trend continues. Where will the food come from? Today the death rate in Costa Rica is low in part because they have a large number of physicians in proportion to their population. How do you suppose those physicians will keep the death rate down when there's not enough food to keep people alive?

One of the most ominous facts of the current situation is that over 40% of the population of the underveloped world is made up of people *under 15 years old*. As that mass of young people moves into its reproductive years during the next decade, we're going to see the greatest baby boom of all time. Those youngsters are the reason for all the ominous predictions for the year 2000. They are the gunpowder for the population explosion.

How did we get into this bind? It all happened a long time ago, and the story involves the process of natural selection, the development of culture, and man's swollen head. The essence of success in evolution is reproduction. Indeed, natural selection is simply defined as differential reproduction of genetic types. That is, if people with blue eyes have more children on the average than those with brown eyes, natural selection is occurring. More genes for blue eyes will be passed on to the next generation than will genes for brown eyes. Should this continue, the population will have progressively larger and larger proportions of blue-eyed people. This differential reproduction of genetic types is the driving force of evolution; it has been driving evolution for billions of years. Whatever types produced more offspring became the common types. Virtually all populations contain very many different genetic types (for reasons that need not concern us), and some are always outreproducing others. As I said, reproduction is the key to winning the evolutionary game. Any structure, physiological process, or pattern of behavior that leads to greater reproductive success will tend to be perpetuated. The entire process by which man developed involves thousands of millennia of our ancestors being more successful breeders than their relatives. Facet number one of our bind—the urge to reproduce has been fixed in us by billions of years of evolution.

Of course through all those years of evolution, our ancestors were fighting a continual battle to keep the birth rate ahead of the death rate. That they were successful is attested to by our very existence, for, if the death rate had overtaken the birth rate for any substantial period of time, the evolutionary line leading to man would have gone extinct. Among our apelike ancestors, a few million years ago, it was very difficult for a mother to rear her children successfully. Most of the offspring died before they reached reproductive age. The death rate was near the birth rate. Then another factor entered the picture—cultural evolution was added to biological evolution.

Culture can be loosely defined as the body of non-genetic information which people pass from generation to generation. It is the accumulated knowledge that, in the old days, was passed on entirely by word of mouth, painting, and demonstration. Several thousand years ago the written word was added to the means of cultural transmission. Today culture is passed on in these ways, and also through television, computer tapes, motion pictures, records, blueprints, and other media. Culture is all the information man possesses except for that which is stored in the chemical language of his genes.

The large size of the human brain evolved in response to the development of cultural information. A big brain is an advantage when dealing with such information. Big-brained individuals were able to deal more successfully with the culture of their group. They were thus more successful reproductively than their smaller-brained relatives. They passed on their genes for big brains to their numerous offspring. They also added to the accumulating store of cultural information, increasing slightly the premium placed on brain size in the next generation. A self-reinforcing selective trend developed —a trend toward increased brain size.[11]

But there was, quite literally, a rub. Babies had bigger and bigger heads. There were limits to how large a woman's pelvis could conveniently become. To make a long story short, the strategy of evolution was not to make a woman bell-shaped and relatively immobile, but to accept the problem of having babies who were helpless for a long period while their brains grew after birth.[12] How could the mother defend and care for her infant during its unusually long period of helplessness? She couldn't, unless Papa hung around. The girls are still working on that problem, but an essential step was to get rid of the short, well-defined breeding season characteristic of most mammals. The year-round sexuality of the human female, the long period of infant dependence on the female, the evolution of the family group, all are at the roots of our present problem. They are essential ingredients in the vast social phenomenon that we call sex. Sex is not simply an act leading to the production of offspring. It is a varied and complex cultural phenomenon penetrating into all aspects of our lives—one involving our self-esteem, our choice of friends, cars, and leaders. It is tightly interwoven with our mythologies and history. Sex in human beings is necessary for the production of young, but it also evolved to ensure their successful rearing. Facet number two of our bind—our urge to reproduce is hopelessly entwined with most of our other urges.

Of course, in the early days the whole system did not prevent a very high mortality among the young, as well as among the older members of the group. Hunting and food-gathering is a risky business. Cavemen had to throw very impressive cave bears out of their caves before people could move in. Witch doctors and shamans had a less than perfect record at treating wounds and curing disease. Life was short, if not sweet. Man's total population size doubtless increased slowly but steadily as human populations expanded out of the African cradle of our species.

Then about 10,000 years ago a major change occurred—the agricultural revolution. People began to give up hunting food and settled down to grow it. Suddenly some of the risk was removed from life. The chances of dying of starvation diminished greatly in some human groups. Other threats associated with the nomadic life were also reduced, perhaps balanced by new threats of disease and large-scale warfare associated with the development of cities. But the overall result was a more secure existence than before, and the human population grew more rapidly. Around 1800, when the standard of living in what are today the ODCs was dramatically increasing due to industrialization, population growth really began to accelerate. The development of medical science was the straw that broke the camel's back. While lowering death rates in the ODCs was due in part to other factors, there is no question that "instant death control," exported by the ODCs, has been responsible for the drastic lowering of death rates in the UDCs. Medical science, with its efficient public health programs, has been able to depress the death rate with astonishing rapidity and at the same time drastically increase the birth rate; healthier people have more babies.

The power of exported death control can best be seen by an examination of the classic case of Ceylon's assault on malaria after World War II. Between 1933 and 1942 the death rate due directly to malaria was *reported* as almost two per thousand. This rate, however, represented only a portion of the malaria deaths, as many were reported as being due to "pyrexia."[13] Indeed, in 1934–1935 a malaria epidemic may have been directly responsible for fully half of the deaths on the island. In addition, malaria, which infected a large portion of the population, made people susceptible to many other diseases. It thus contributed to the death rate indirectly as well as directly.

The introduction of DDT in 1946 brought rapid control over the mosquitoes which carry malaria. As a result, the death rate on the island was halved in less than a decade. The death rate in Ceylon in 1945 was 22. It dropped 34% between 1946 and 1947 and moved down to ten in 1954. Since the sharp postwar drop it has continued to decline and now stands at eight. Although part of the drop is doubtless due to the killing of other insects which carry disease and to other public health measures, most of it can be accounted for by the control of malaria.

Victory over malaria, yellow fever, smallpox, cholera, and other infectious diseases has been responsible for similar plunges in death rate throughout most of the UDCs. In the decade 1940–1950 the death rate declined 46% in Puerto Rico, 43% in Formosa, and 23% in Jamaica. In a sample of 18 undeveloped areas the average decline in death rate between 1945 and 1950 was 24%.

It is, of course, socially very acceptable to reduce the death rate. Billions of years of evolution have given us all a powerful will to live. Intervening in the birth rate goes against our evolutionary values. During all those centuries of our evolutionary past, the individuals who had the most children passed on their genetic endowment in greater quantities than those who reproduced less. Their genes dominate our heredity today. All our biological urges are for more reproduction, and they are all too often reinforced by our culture. In brief, death control goes with the grain, birth control against it.

In summary, the world's population will continue to grow as long as the birth rate exceeds the death rate; it's as simple as that. When it stops growing or starts to shrink, it will mean that either the birth rate has gone down or the death rate has gone up or a combination of the two. Basically, then, there are only two kinds of solutions to the population problem. One is a "birth rate solution," in which we find ways to lower the birth rate. The other is a "death rate solution," in which ways to raise the death rate—war, famine, pestilence—*find us.* The problem could have been avoided by *population control,* in which mankind consciously adjusted the birth rate so that a "death rate solution" did not have to occur.

Too Little Food

Why did I pick on the next nine years instead of the next 900 for finding a solution to the population crisis? One answer is that the world is rapidly running out of food. And famine, of course, could be one way to reach a death rate solution to the population problem. In fact, the battle to feed humanity is already lost, in the sense that we will not be able to prevent large-scale famines in the next decade or so. It is difficult to guess what the exact scale and consequences of the famines will be. But there *will be* famines. Let's look at the situation today.

At least half of the people of the world are now undernourished (have too little food) or malnourished (have serious imbalances in their diet). The number of deaths attributable to starvation is open to considerable debate. The reason is threefold. First, demographic statistics are often incomplete or unreliable. Second, starving people usually don't die of starvation. They often fall victim to some disease as they weaken. When good medical care is available, starvation can be a long, drawn-out process indeed. Third, and perhaps most important, starvation is undramatic. Deaths from starvation go unnoticed, even when they occur as close as Mississippi. Many Americans are under the delusion that an Asian can live happily "on a bowl of rice a day." Such a diet means slow starvation for an Asian, just as it would for an American. A *New Republic* article[14] estimated that five million Indian children die each year of malnutrition. Dumont and Rosier in their book *The Hungry Future*[15] estimate that 10 to 20 million people will starve to death this year, mostly children. Senator George McGovern[16] has called hunger "the chief killer of man."

Through the first decade following World War II, food production per person in the UDCs kept up with population growth. Then, sometime around 1958, "the stork passed the plow."[17] Serious transfers of food began from the ODCs to the UDCs. As food got scarcer, economic laws of supply and demand began to take effect in the UDCs. Food prices began to rise. Marginal land began to be brought into production—as evidenced by reduced yields per acre. In short, all the signs of an approaching food crisis began to appear. Then in 1965–1966 came the first dramatic blow.

In 1965–1966 mankind suffered a shocking defeat in what is now popularly called the "war on hunger." In 1966, while the population of the world increased by some 70 million people, there was *no* compensatory increase in food production. According to the United Nations Food and Agriculture Organization (FAO), advances in food production made in developing nations between 1955 and 1965 were wiped out by agricultural disasters in 1965 and 1966. In 1966 each person on Earth had 2% less to eat, the reduction, of course, not being uniformly distributed. Only ten countries grew more food than they consumed: the United States, Canada, Australia, Argentina, France, New Zealand, Burma, Thailand, Rumania, and South Africa. The United States produced more than half of the surplus, with Canada and Australia contributing most of the balance. All other countries, including the giants of China, India, and Russia, imported more than they exported. In 1966 the United States shipped *one quarter* of its wheat crop, nine million tons, to India. In the process we helped change the distribution of people in the country. Thousands migrated into port cities so as to be close to the centers of wheat distribution. We also, in the opinion of some, hindered India's own agricultural development. Perhaps we gave too many Indians the impression that we have an unlimited capacity to ship them food. Unhappily, we do not.

In 1967 we were extremely fortunate in having a fine growing year almost worldwide; harvests almost reached the per capita level of 1964. This partial recovery, due largely to good weather, shifted some agriculturists (especially in the U.S. Department of Agriculture) from pessimism to limited optimism about the world food situation. Some hopeful signs, especially in the form of new wheat and rice varieties (the Green Revolution), encouraged even more optimism. But even those most concerned with the Green Revolution say it can at the very best buy us only a decade or two in which to try to stop population growth. It's too soon to evaluate its true potential. But it clearly cannot be assigned the panacea role so devoutly wished for by many.

Even with the Green Revolution well established in some areas, there was again *no* increase in world food production during 1969 according to the FAO, while the population inexorably rose by 2%. Much of the lack of increase was due to deliberately lower production in ODCs, which in 1968 had produced great grain surpluses that they were unable to sell. These were economic surpluses, food that destitute, hungry people in other countries could not buy. The possibility that such "surpluses" can exist is in itself a commentary on the moral conscience and economic system of the world.

Large segments of the populations of many UDCs (and many people in some ODCs) simply do not receive enough to eat. If the world's food were equitably distributed (which it certainly isn't today),[18] there would be enough calories—just barely—for everyone. Some

THE PROBLEM   21

optimists maintain that there is plenty of food and that
food will not be a problem in the future. Usually, these
people are only counting calories. Unfortunately, human
beings need much more than calories to stay alive and
healthy; they need protein, fats, vitamins, and minerals.
Malnutrition—a lack of one or more of these essential
elements in the diet—is even more widespread than a
shortage of calories. The most common deficiency is in
protein. Without enough high-quality protein (protein
which is properly constituted to meet human nutritional
requirements) in a mother's diet during pregnancy and
in a child's diet during the first few years, the child may
suffer permanent brain impairment and be mentally
retarded. Permanent dwarfing, crippling, and blindness
(as well as illness and death) can also result from various nutritional deficiencies.

So the food problem is not simply one of providing
more food. The *quality* of food provided is also very
important. Protein is the key to the world food problem
—it is high-quality protein which is most expensive to
obtain, both in economic terms and in terms of the
ecological cost of getting it. The highest quality and
highest concentrations of protein are found in meat, sea-
food, poultry, and animal products such as milk and
eggs. Poor people must subsist mainly on plant foods—
grains, fruits, and vegetables—thus their diets may have
inadequate protein, both in amount and quality.

Some of the most depressing situations are found in
Latin America. There, politicians have generally been
far behind those of Asia in recognizing overpopulation
as a major source of their problems. As noted earlier,
doubling times in many Latin American countries are
truly spectacular. And the poverty, hunger, and misery
of the people are equally spectacular. The hideous conditions in the urban slums—*favelas* in Brazil, *barriadas*
in Peru, *tugurios* in Colombia, *ranchos* in Venezuela—
have received wide publicity in the press and popular

magazines in recent years. Yet most Americans either do not know or choose to ignore the true depths of the misery and despair in which so many of our southern neighbors spin out their lives. Dry figures unfortunately make little impression. It is hard to grasp the meaning of Peru's doubling time of 23 years. It is easy, however, to grasp the meaning of Peruvian Indian children chewing coca leaves. The leaves are the source of cocaine, which suppresses the children's hunger pains.

Turning to Colombia, we find an extremely poor country with a doubling time of 21 years. Death control did not reach Colombia until after World War II. Before it arrived, a woman could expect to have two or three children survive to reproductive age if she went through ten pregnancies. Now, in spite of malnutrition, medical technology keeps seven or eight alive. Each child adds to the impossible financial burden of the family and to the despair of the mother. According to Dr. Sumner M. Kalman,[19] the average mother goes through a progression of attempts to limit the size of her family. She starts with ineffective native forms of contraception and moves on to quack abortion, infanticide, frigidity, and all too often to suicide. That's the kind of misery that's concealed behind the dry statistic of a population doubling every 21 years. What do you suppose American families would do if, after the last child was born, the average family had to spend 80% of its income on food? That's the spot the Colombians are in.

Arthur Hopcraft has published a book, *Born to Hunger*,[20] which might be described as a "report from the front" of the war on hunger. His record of a 45,000-mile trip through Africa, Asia, and South America has much greater immediacy than any set of population-food production statistics. He visited a Dr. Lema, whose survey of the vicinity of Dar es Salaam, Tanzania, revealed 30% of the children under five to be malnourished. Sixty-five of those children were hospitalized with severe kwashiorkor, a malnutrition disease "in which open sores spread over the flesh, particularly on the thighs and lower body, so that the child looks as if he had been badly burned." Fourteen of these children died. To the west of Dar es Salaam, in a less fertile region, the death rate of children under five is nearly 50%. Hopcraft quotes Dr. Shah of Ajarpura, India, to the effect that the infant mortality rate of 125 per 1,000 births in the area was due to gastroenteritis, respiratory diseases, and malnutrition. Ajarpura was considered a progressive village, although the majority of the people were malnourished.

From Colombia, Hopcraft reports 100 infant deaths *per day* from malnutrition, supporting the picture of desperation painted by Kalman. From Turkana, Kenya, he reports 6,000 people still living on handouts in famine camps established in 1961. Hopcraft reminds us again of what we must never forget as we contemplate our unprecedented problems—that in all the mess of expanding population, faltering food production, and environmental deterioration are enmeshed miserable, hungry, desperate human beings.

I wish I could tell you that in the face of this dilemma the United States is doing everything it possibly can to help the less fortunate people of our globe. Quite the contrary; in many ways we have been a major factor in pushing them into deeper misery. We have cooperated in a "rich man's club" of nations which has controlled the world trade situation to the great detriment of the UDCs. Along with the other ODCs, we have grabbed the lion's share of the world's protein—taking more from the protein-starved citizens of the UDCs than we return to them. What's worse, we feed a great deal of the protein we import to our pets (that protein is lost forever as human food) and to our farm animals (50% to 90% of that protein is lost to mankind).

Perhaps worst of all, in order to protect our overseas

commercial empire and to protect our access to the resources we "need" for our affluent society, the United States has supported an unhappy status quo throughout the "Third World." We have backed a series of dictators and oligarchs in numerous countries under a phoney banner of "anti-Communism." By open and covert action we have often prevented land reform and other socio-political changes which are needed before reasonable agricultural development can occur.[21] There is no question that changing this pattern of behavior will be essential to the survival of both UDCs and ODCs; the world can no longer afford to support and tolerate such inequities.

Soon food production in the UDCs will fall catastrophically behind population growth. Many of these countries now rely heavily on imports. As the crisis deepens, where will the imports come from? Not from Russia—she herself will probably need to import food. Not from Canada, Argentina, or Australia. They need money and will be busy selling to food-short countries, such as Russia, which can afford to buy. From the United States then?

They will get some, perhaps, but not anywhere near enough. Our vast agricultural surpluses are long gone. Indeed, if we were to suffer a large-scale crop failure, we would be in serious trouble. We have less than one year's supply of stored crops. Our agriculture is already highly efficient, so the prospects of massively increasing our production are dim. And the problems of food transport are vast. No knowledgeable person thinks that the United States can save the world from famine with food exports, although we might be of considerable help in temporary or local situations which may precede a general collapse.

All of this can be easily summarized. There is not enough food today. How much there will be tomorrow is open to debate. If the optimists are correct, today's level of misery will be perpetuated for perhaps two decades into the future. If the pessimists are correct, massive famines will occur soon, possibly in the 1970s, certainly by the early 1980s. So far most of the evidence seems to be on the side of the pessimists, and we should plan on the assumption that they are correct. After all, some two billion people aren't being properly fed in 1971!

A Dying Planet

Our problems would be much simpler if we needed only to consider the balance between food and population. But in the long view the progressive deterioration of our environment may cause more death and misery than the food-population gap. And it is just this factor, environmental deterioration, that is almost universally ignored by those most concerned with closing the food gap.

It is fair to say that the environment of every organism, human and nonhuman, on the face of the Earth has been influenced by the population explosion of *Homo sapiens*. As direct or indirect results of this explosion, some organisms, such as the passenger pigeon, are now extinct. Many others, such as the larger wild animals of all continents, have been greatly reduced in numbers. Still others, such as sewer rats and house flies, enjoy much enlarged populations. But these are obvious results and probably less important than more subtle changes in the complex web of life and in delicately balanced natural chemical cycles. Ecologists—those biologists who study the relationships of plants and animals with their environments—are especially concerned about these changes. They realize how easily disrupted are ecological systems (called ecosystems), and they are afraid of both the short- and long-range consequences for these eco-systems of many of mankind's activities.

Environmental changes connected with agriculture are often striking. For instance, in the United States we are paying a price for maintaining our high level of food production. Professor LaMonte Cole has written,[22] ". . . even our own young country is not immune to deterioration. We have lost many thousands of acres to erosion and gullying, and many thousands more to strip mining. It has been estimated that the agricultural value of Iowa farmland, which is about as good land as we have, is declining by 1% per year. In our irrigated lands of the West there is the constant danger of salinization from rising water tables, while, elsewhere, from Long Island to Southern California, we have lowered water tables so greatly that in coastal regions salt water is seeping into the aquifers. Meanwhile, an estimated two thousand irrigation dams in the United States are now useless impoundments of silt, sand, and gravel."

The history of similar deterioration in other parts of the world is clear for those who know how to read it. It stretches back to the cradles of civilization in the Middle East, where in many places deserts now occupy what were once rich and productive farmlands. In this area the process of destruction goes on today as in the past, still having ecologically incompetent use of water resources as a major feature. A good example is the building of dams on the Nile, preventing the deposit of nutrient-rich silt that used to accompany annual floods of the river. As almost anyone who remembers his high-school geography could have predicted, the result has been a continuing decrease in the productivity of soils in the Nile Delta. As Cole put it, "The new Aswan high dam is designed to bring another million acres of land under irrigation, and it may well prove to be the ultimate disaster for Egypt." The proposed damming of the Me-kong could produce the same results for Vietnam and her neighbors.

The present growth of the world population commits us irrevocably to a policy of increasing annual food production for at least the next two or three generations. If this is to be successful, we must learn to do it in the most efficient, least damaging way. If we want the most food produced per acre, we must for the most part eat the plants. The reason is quite simple: the Second Law of Thermodynamics. The law says, in part, that when energy is transferred, some of it becomes unusable at each transfer. Each time energy is transferred in an ecosystem, some of it is converted into heat energy which is not usable by the organisms in the system.

Consider a simple example of what ecologists call a "food chain." A plant is eaten by an insect which is eaten by a trout which in turn is eaten by you. The plant has bound some of the energy of the sun in the chemical bonds of its molecules. The insect extracts that energy and uses some of it to make insect tissues. The trout, in turn, extracts some of the energy in the insect and uses some of it to make trout. Finally, you extract some of the energy in the trout and make it into *Homo sapiens*. In transfers of this type only 10–20% of the energy present in what was eaten at stage one turns up as usable energy at stage two. To put it another way (using the lower efficiency figure), 1,000 calories of plant makes 100 calories of insect which makes ten calories of trout which makes one calorie of person. By skipping the insect and trout links in the food chain, we could get 1,000 calories input simply by eating the plant ourselves, rather than settling for ten calories of trout. Similarly, 100 calories of grain suitable for human consumption but fed to cattle produce at most 10 to 20 calories worth of beef.

For this reason, as the world gets hungrier, we will feed lower and lower on the food chains, meat will get more and more expensive, and most of us will become vegetarians. Meat will not disappear entirely, however. Many semi-arid areas which cannot be irrigated and farmed will support grazing. Similarly, for the foreseeable future, most of the nourishment we extract from the sea will be in the form of meat.

Plans for increasing food production, such as the Green Revolution, invariably involve large-scale efforts at environmental modification. These plans involve the "inputs" so beloved of the agricultural propagandist—especially inorganic fertilizers to enrich soils and synthetic pesticides to discourage our competitors. The new strains of wheat and rice require large amounts of fertilizer and more irrigation water than traditional ones do in order to produce their high yields. Their resistance to pests is unknown; they may also need higher inputs of pesticides for protection. Growing more food also may involve the clearing of forests from additional land and the provision of irrigation water. There seems to be little hope that we will suddenly have an upsurge in the level of responsibility or ecological sophistication of persons concerned with increasing agricultural output. I predict that the rate of soil deterioration will accelerate as the food crisis intensifies. Ecology will be ignored more and more as things get tough. It is safe to assume that our use of synthetic pesticides, already massive, will continue to increase, especially in UDCs. In spite of much publicity, the intimate relationship between pesticides on the one hand and environmental deterioration on the other is not often recognized. This relationship is well worth a close look.

One of the basic facts of population biology—that branch of biology that deals with groups of organisms—is that the simpler an ecosystem is, the more unstable it is. A complex forest, consisting of a great variety of plants and animals, will persist year in and year out (with no interference from man). The system contains many elements, and changes in different elements often cancel each other out. Suppose one kind of predator eating mice and rabbits suffers a population decline. For instance, suppose most of the foxes in the forest die of disease? The role of that predator will probably be assumed by another, perhaps weasels or owls. There is no population explosion of mice or rabbits. Such compensation may not be possible in a simpler ecosystem. Similarly, no plant-eating animal (herbivore) feeds on all kinds of plants. So the chance of one kind of herbivore, in a population explosion, completely devouring all the leaves in a mixed woodland is virtually nil.

Man, however, is a simplifier of complex ecosystems and a creator of simple ecosystems. Synthetic pesticides, for instance, are one of man's most potent tools for reducing the complexity of ecosystems. Insects which we consider to be pests are most often herbivores: corn earworms, potato beetles, boll weevils, cabbage butterflies, etc. Herbivores ordinarily have larger populations than the meat-eaters (carnivores) which feed on them. There are many more deer than there are mountain lions. Those animals with the largest populations are also those most likely to become genetically resistant to assault with pesticides. The reason is not complicated. The original large populations are just more likely to contain the relatively rare genetic varieties which are already resistant. Individuals of these varieties will survive and breed, and their offspring will be resistant.

There is a second reason why herbivores are more likely to become genetically resistant to pesticides. For millions of years the plants have been fighting them with their own pesticides. Many of the sharp flavors of spices come from chemicals that plants have evolved to poison or repel the insects which are eating them. The insects in turn, have evolved ways of protecting themselves from the poisons. So the herbivorous insects have been fighting the pesticide war for many millions of years—no wonder they're so good at it.

What happens when a complex ecosystem is treated with a synthetic pesticide? Some of the carnivorous species are exterminated, and the pests become resistant. The ecosystem is simplified by the removal of the carnivores and becomes less stable. Since carnivores can no longer help control the size of the pest population, the pesticide treatments must be escalated to more and more dangerous levels. Ads for insecticides sometimes imply that there is some absolute number of pests—that if we could just eliminate all the "public enemies" things would be dandy. In fact, pesticides often *create* pests. Careless overuse of DDT has promoted to "pest" category many species of mites, little insectlike relatives of spiders. The insects which ate the mites were killed by the DDT, and the mites were resistant to DDT. There you have it—instant pests, and more profits for the agricultural chemical industry in fighting these Frankensteins of their own creation. What's more, some of the more potent miticides the chemists have developed with which to do battle seem to be powerful carcinogens— cancer-producing substances.

When man creates simple ecosystems, he automatically creates ecological problems for himself. For instance, he often plants stands of a single grass—wheat fields and corn fields are familiar examples. These lack the complexity necessary for stability and so are subject to almost instant ruination when not guarded constantly. They are particularly vulnerable because very often the natural anti-insect chemicals have been selected out of the crop plant by plant breeders (these chemicals often don't taste good to us, either!).

Pesticides, of course, also reduce the diversity of life in the soil. Remember, soil is not just crushed rock and decaying organic matter. It contains myriads of tiny plants, animals, and microbes, which are essential to its fertility. Damage from pesticides must be added to all of the other sources of soil deterioration active today.

Of all the synthetic organic pesticides, we probably know the most about DDT. It is the oldest and most widely used chlorinated hydrocarbon insecticide. It is not found only where it has been applied. Virtually all populations of animals the world over are contaminated with it. DDT tends to accumulate in fatty tissues. Concentrations in the fat deposits of Americans average 11 parts per million (ppm), and Israelis have been found to have as much as 19.2 ppm. More significant in some ways has been the discovery of DDT residues in such unlikely places as the fat deposits of Eskimos, Antarctic penguins, and Antarctic seals. Seals from the east coast of Scotland have been found with concentrations as high as 23 ppm in their blubber. Pesticide pollution is truly a worldwide problem.

In nature DDT breaks down very slowly. It will last for decades in soils. A study of a Long Island marsh that had been sprayed for 20 years for mosquito control revealed up to 32 pounds per acre of DDT in the upper layer of mud.[23] Unhappily, the way DDT circulates in ecosystems leads to a concentration in carnivores; it is concentrated as it is passed along a food chain. While most of the food energy is lost at each transfer up the food chain, most of the DDT is retained. The danger to life and the reproductive capacity of some meat-eating birds is approaching a critical stage now, and the outlook for man if current trends continue does not seem healthy. The day may come when the obese people of the world must give up diets, since metabolizing their fat deposits will lead to DDT poisoning. But, on the bright side, it is clear that fewer and fewer people in the future will be obese! We must remember that DDT has been in use for only about a quarter of a century. It is difficult to predict the results of another 25 years of application of DDT and similar compounds, especially if those years are to be filled with frantic attempts to feed more and more people, but the harm seems likely to outweigh the benefits more and more as time goes on.

Concern about the effects of our ecologically incompetent use of synthetic pesticides has been widespread for years, and many environmental biologists have spoken out in warning. Perhaps the most famous was Rachel Carson, whose splendid *Silent Spring* became a best seller. I would also highly recommend Robert L. Rudd's more technical *Pesticides and the Living Landscape* and Frank Graham's *Since Silent Spring,*[24] which covers more recent events. But those financially involved in the massive production and application of pesticides seem to have only one reaction. They and their hired hands among entomologists heap ridicule and abuse upon the ecologists.

Unfortunately, of course, there are some dietary extremists and the "no-pesticide-ever-for-any-reason" school which provide ammunition to the pesticide industry, but that doesn't change the facts of the case. It is probably true that the direct and immediate threat to human health in present-day use of synthetic pesticides is not extreme. It is also true that many people have led longer, healthier lives because of pesticides—as in Ceylon. The question of long-term effects on health remains open, however. They are difficult to judge until the long term has passed. Recent studies have shown a relationship between deaths due to certain liver diseases and stress diseases and higher than average concentrations of DDT in corpses.[25] Individuals born since 1945, and thus exposed to DDT since before birth, may well have shorter life expectancies than they would if DDT had never existed. We won't know until the first of these reach their forties and fifties. Since the experiment is being run on the entire world, we may never know exactly how much difference it has made.

Present-day practices can be condemned on several

other counts. First of all, they are often basically un-
economical, locking the farmer and other users into
expensive programs that could be avoided by using
ecologically more sophisticated control methods and by
reeducating the public. For instance, housewives should
be taught to accept certain levels of insect damage in
their produce in lieu of the small dose of poison they
now get. Secondly, and by far most importantly, there
are the simplifying effects on ecosystems discussed
above, effects which in many cases may now be
irreversible.

One could go on with pesticide horror stories galore.
The scientific literature is replete with them. There are
stories of dying birds, of mosquito fishes resistant to
endrin (a potent insecticide) and excreting so much of
the chemical that they kill nonresistant fishes kept in the
same aquarium. It is a record of ecological stupidity
without parallel.

One specific episode will illustrate how complex and
subtle the effects may be. Professor L. B. Slobodkin[26]
has described a plan to block the seaward ends of lochs
in western Scotland and use them as ponds for raising
fishes. One of the problems has been to find ways to
raise the young fishes in the laboratory so that they can
be "planted" in the ponds. It has been discovered that
newly hatched brine shrimp serve as a satisfactory food
for the kind of fishes that will be raised. These may
be obtained from brine shrimp eggs that are gathered
commercially in the United States and sold to tropical
fish fanciers for use in feeding young tropical fishes. The
American supplies come from two places—the San
Francisco Bay Area and the Great Salt Lake Basin in
Utah. Sufficient eggs for the project can no longer be
obtained from the Bay Area because of the demands of
the aquarists, and because large areas of suitable brine
shrimp habitat are now subdivisions. Unfortunately,
the Utah supply is no use to the British since brine

shrimp hatched from Utah eggs kill their young fishes. The poisonous quality of the Utah shrimp comes from insecticide residues draining from farmlands in the region. So insecticide pollution in Utah is blocking fish production in Scotland!

Finally, pesticides contribute to the serious problems of general environmental pollution. Professor Cole[27] warned, "It is true that 70% or more of the total oxygen production by photosynthesis occurs in the ocean and is largely produced by planktonic diatoms. It is also true that we are dumping into the oceans vast quantities of pollutants consisting, according to one estimate by the U. S. Food and Drug Administration, of as many as a half-million substances. Many of these are biologically active materials, such as pesticides, radioisotopes, and detergents, to which the Earth's living forms have never before had to try to adapt. No more than a minute fraction of these substances and combinations of them has been tested for toxicity to marine diatoms, or, for that matter, to the equally vital forms of life involved in the cycles of nitrogen and other essential elements. I do not think we are in a position to assert right now that we are not poisoning the marine diatoms and thus bringing disaster upon ourselves."

Since Cole wrote these words, an article in *Science* magazine[28] has described reduced photosynthesis in laboratory studies of marine diatoms exposed to DDT. We are, of course, removing many terrestrial areas from oxygen production by paving them. We are also depleting the world's supply of oxygen by burning (oxidizing) vast quantities of fossil fuels and by clearing iron-rich tropical soils in which the iron is then oxidized. When the rate of oxygen consumption exceeds the rate at which it is produced, then the oxygen content of the atmosphere will decrease. As Cole says, "If this [decrease] occurred gradually, its effect would be approximately the same as moving everyone to higher altitudes, a change that might help to alleviate the population crisis by raising death rates."

However, photosynthesis by the present plant population of the Earth produces a yearly quantity of oxygen equivalent to only a tiny fraction of the mass of oxygen already accumulated in the atmosphere. If we drastically reduce photosynthesis, oxygen depletion will occur, but probably very slowly. I suspect that other ecological catastrophes accompanying poisoning of the sea and clearing plants from the land would lead to mankind's extinction long before we have to start worrying about running out of oxygen. For example, DDT affects some kinds of planktonic plants more than others. This could lead to large changes in the plant plankton communities which are the basic source of energy for marine life. The results for our fisheries could be catastrophic. Therefore food depletion probably would be the first and most obvious effect of poisoning the tiny plants of the sea.

If you live in one of our great metropolitan areas, you know very well that pesticides are just one of many factors in the pollution of our planet. The mixture of filth that is dignified with the label "air" in places like Los Angeles, St. Louis, and New York would not have been tolerated by citizens of those cities 50 years ago. But clean air gradually changed to smog, and nobody paid much attention. Sadly, man's evolution did not provide him with a nervous system that readily detects changes that take place slowly, not in minutes, hours, or days, but over decades. It was important for early man and his nonhuman ancestors to be able to detect rather sudden changes in their environments. The caveman who did not immediately notice the appearance of a cave bear did not survive to pass on his genes for a dull-witted nervous system. Large animals charging, rocks falling, children crying, fires starting—these are the sort of short-range changes that our ancestors had to react to. But the world of 276,824 B.C. was much like that of 276,804 B.C. There was little reason for a creature that only lived an average of perhaps 20 years to learn to deal with environmental changes that occurred over decades. We perceive sudden changes readily, slow changes with difficulty.

If the smog had appeared in Los Angeles overnight, people would have fled gibbering into the hills. But it came on gradually, and man, adaptable organism that he is, learned to live with it. We first paid serious attention to smog when it presented itself as a direct health hazard. Smog disasters years ago in Donora, Pennsylvania, and London, England, produced dead bodies and thus attracted attention. Corpses usually are required to attract the attention of those who pooh-pooh environmental threats—indeed many of my colleagues feel that only a pesticide disaster of large magnitude will produce a real measure of rational control over these substances. The 1952 London incident was blamed for 4,000 deaths, the current record. Since then a clear link between air pollution and respiratory disease has been established. For instance, doctors compared cigarette smokers from smoggy St. Louis with cigarette smokers from relatively smog-free Winnipeg, Canada. There was roughly four times as much emphysema—an extremely unpleasant disease that suffocates its victims—among the group from St. Louis. Death rates from both emphysema and lung cancer have risen spectacularly over the last decade, especially among urban populations. Pollution also may be linked with certain kinds of heart disease and tuberculosis, not as a cause but as a contributor to higher death rates. In addition to this disease threat there is also the strong suspicion that occurrence of certain cancers is associated with specific pollutants in the air. People now are generally aware of the air pollution problem, at least as far as its direct challenges to health and beauty are concerned. But, once again, the subtle and much more important ecological threats usually remain unrecognized.

One such threat, of course, comes from the killing of plants, many of which have little resistance to smog. Remember, every plant that goes is one less contributor to our food and oxygen supplies. But even more important is the potential for changing the climate of the Earth. All of the junk we dump into the atmosphere, all of the dust, all of the carbon dioxide, have effects on the temperature balance of the Earth. Air pollution affects how much of the sun's heat reaches the surface of the Earth and how much is radiated back into space. And it is just this temperature balance that causes the changes in the atmosphere that we call "the weather."

Concern about this problem has been greatly increased by the prospect of supersonic transports. Most people have been opposing this project on the basis that the "sonic booms" generated will drive half the people in the country out of their skulls while benefiting almost no one. But ecologists, as usual, have been looking at the less obvious. Supersonic transports will leave contrails high in the stratosphere, where they will break up very slowly. A lid of ice crystals gradually will be deposited high in the atmosphere, which might add to the "greenhouse effect" (prevention of the heat of the Earth from radiating back into space). On the other hand, they may produce a greater cooling than heating effect because of the sun's rays which they reflect back into space. One way or another, you can bet their effect will not be "neutral." The greenhouse effect is being enhanced now by the greatly increased level of carbon dioxide in the atmosphere. In the last one hundred years our burning of fossil fuels raised the level some 15%. The greenhouse effect today is being countered by low-level clouds generated by contrails, dust, and other contaminants that tend to keep the energy of the sun from warming the surface as much.

At the moment we cannot predict what the overall climatic results will be of our using the atmosphere as a garbage dump. We do know that very small changes in either direction in the average temperature of the Earth could be very serious. With a few degrees of cooling, a new ice age might be upon us, with rapid and drastic effects on the agricultural productivity of the temperate regions. With a few degrees of heating, the Greenland and Antarctic ice caps would melt, perhaps raising ocean levels 250 feet. Gondola to the Empire State Building, anyone?

In short, when we pollute, we tamper with the energy balance of the Earth. The results in terms of global climate and in terms of local weather could be catastrophic. Do we want to keep it up and find out what will happen? What do we gain by playing "environmental roulette"?

My first job after I got my doctorate was working as a research associate with Dr. Joseph H. Camin, then of the Chicago Academy of Sciences. That was in 1957–1958. Ten years later, Joe Camin spent a sabbatical leave with me at Stanford. We reminisced over some extremely pleasant times we had had working together on a field problem, studying natural selection in water snakes which lived on islands in the western end of Lake Erie. The problem was fascinating, and we would be very much interested in continuing the research today. But all we can do is reminisce. You see, Lake Erie has died. The lake can no longer support organisms which require clean, oxygen-rich water. Much of this shallow body of water is a stinking mess—more reminiscent of a septic tank than the beautiful lake it once was. The snakes are almost gone, as are the fishes on which they fed. In 1955 the lake supported commercial fishing for high-quality fish. In that year 75 million pounds of fish were taken. No one in his right mind would eat a Lake Erie fish today.

Lake Erie is just one example of a general problem of pollution of lakes, rivers, and streams in the United States and around the world. Lake Michigan will soon follow it in extinction. A recent *New York Times* article described the reduced chances of Russian conservationists to save Lake Baikal and its unique plant and animal life from a fate similar to that of Lake Erie. Many of the world's rivers are quickly approaching the "too thin to plow and too thick to drink" stage—and carrying to the sea those dangerous compounds discussed above.

Finally, let me mention a pollution problem not limited to air or water. We are constantly adding lead to our environment from ethyl gasoline and pesticides, and it is present also in many common substances such as paints and food-can solder. Some scientists are very much concerned with the quantities of lead found in the bodies of Americans. In some instances these are approaching the levels necessary to produce symptoms of chronic lead poisoning—weakness, apathy, lowered fertility, miscarriage, etc. It is a sobering thought that overexposure to lead was a factor in the decline of the Roman Empire. As Dr. S. C. Gilfillián[29] has pointed out, the Romans lined their bronze cooking, eating, and wine storage vessels with lead. They thus avoided the obvious and unpleasant taste and symptoms of copper poisoning. They traded them for the pleasant flavor and more subtle poisoning associated with lead. Lead was also common in Roman life in the form of paints, and lead pipes often were used to carry water. Examination of the bones of upper-class Romans of the classical period shows high concentrations of lead—possibly one cause of the famous decadence of Roman leadership. The lower classes lived more simply, drank less wine from lead-lined containers, and thus may have picked up far less lead. This little horror study should make us all more leery of the "corpses before we recognize the problem" school of thought. Chronic low-level effects can be critical, too. Recently there have been some moves to reduce the lead intake of Americans by reducing the amount of leaded gasoline used. A virtually complete ban on such gasoline is badly needed.

Other heavy metals are turning up as environmental hazards, notably mercury and cadmium. Both metals are very poisonous and both enter the environment as industrial wastes. The major source of mercury pollution is the process for producing chlorine (large amounts of which are used in the manufacture of plastics). Seed grain is often treated with mercury fungicides, which resulted in the poisoning of an entire family in New Mexico in 1969. Similar accidents have been reported in several countries. Other sources of mercury pollution are pulp mills, hospitals, and laboratories.

Mercury occurs in both inorganic and organic forms, the latter being somewhat more toxic, resulting in brain damage. Exactly how much mercury will produce overt symptoms of poisoning has not been determined. Moreover, as with lead, low-level chronic doses may well have detrimental effects. High concentrations of mercury have been found in numerous kinds of fish and wildlife in and around North American rivers and lakes and in other ODCs where tests have been made. In these heavily polluted waterways, large quantities of mercury have accumulated, which are gradually being converted by microorganisms to the dangerous organic form, methyl mercury. Methyl mercury easily enters food chains. Even if no more mercury is discharged into these waters, enough is stored on the bottom in some areas to keep adding methyl mercury to local food chains for centuries. Mercury is, of course, poisonous to other organisms as well as human beings. It has been found to reduce photosynthesis in planktonic plants,[30] as does DDT. Recently, concentrations well above FDA acceptable levels have been found in tuna fish and swordfish sold for food in the U.S. Both fish come from the open sea; it appears that mercury is another worldwide pollution problem. How serious it is we are only beginning to discover.

Obviously, the use of mercury in industrial processes and in seed preservatives should be stopped wherever possible. In situations where it can't be replaced by something else, it should not be allowed to escape into the environment. If it becomes feasible, every effort should be made to remove or inactivate the accumulated mercury from freshwater systems.

Deterioration of our environment clearly holds threats for our physical well-being, present and future. What about our mental health? Does the deterioration threaten it, too? Are we living in a deteriorating "psychic environment"? Riots, rising crime rates, disaffection of youth, and increased drug usage seem to indicate that we are. Unfortunately, we can't even be sure how much of the reaction of an individual to the deterioration of his environment is hereditarily conditioned, or how much is a product of his culture. At least three biologists, H. H. Iltis, P. Andrews, and O. L. Loucks[31] feel that nature as well as nurture may be very important, that mankind's genetic endowment has been shaped by evolution to require "natural" surroundings for optimum mental health. These biologists write:

"Unique as we may think we are, we are nevertheless as likely to be genetically programed to a natural habitat of clean air and a varied green landscape as any other mammal. To be relaxed and feel healthy usually means simply allowing our bodies to react in the way for which one hundred millions of years of evolution has equipped us. Physically and genetically, we appear best adapted to a tropical savanna, but as a cultural animal we utilize learned adaptations to cities and towns. For thousands of years we have tried in our houses to imitate not only the climate, but the setting of our evolutionary past: warm, humid air, green plants, and even animal companions. Today, if we can afford it, we may even build a greenhouse or swimming pool next to our living room, buy a place in the country, or at least take our children vacationing on the seashore. The specific physiological reactions to natural beauty and diversity, to the shapes and colors of nature (especially to green), to the motions and sounds of other animals, such as birds, we as yet do not comprehend. But it is evident that nature in our daily life should be thought of as a part of the biological need. It cannot be neglected in the discussions of resource policy for man."

You will note that my discussion of man's environment has not dwelt on the themes that characterize the pleas of conservationists. I haven't discussed the rumor that a giant vinyl redwood tree will be constructed and trucked around the State of California for all to see (permitting all the other "useless" redwoods to be mowed down by our progressive lumbering industry). I've shed no tears here for the passenger pigeons, now extinct, or the California condors, soon to join them. No tears for them, or for the great auk, or the mammoths, or the great herds of bison, or the California grizzly bears, or the Carolina parakeet. I haven't written about them, or of the pleasantness, beauty, indeed glory of many natural areas. Instead I have concentrated on things that seem to bear most directly on man. The reason is simple. In spite of all the efforts of conservationists, all the propaganda, all the eloquent writing, all the beautiful pictures, the conservation battle is presently being lost. In my years of interest in this question I've come to the conclusion that it is being lost for two powerful reasons. The first, of course, is that nothing "undeveloped" can long stand in the face of the population explosion. The second is that most Americans clearly don't give a damn. They've never heard of the California condor and would shed no tears if it became extinct. On the contrary, many Americans would compete for the privilege of shooting the last one. Our population consists of two groups; a comparatively small one dedicated to the preservation of beauty and wild-life, and a vastly larger one dedicated to the destruction of both (or at least apathetic toward them). I am assuming that the first group is with me and that the second cannot be moved to action by an appeal to beauty, or a plea for mercy for what may well be our only living companions in a vast universe.

I have just scratched the surface of the problem of environmental deterioration, but I hope that I have at least convinced you that subtle ecological effects may be much more important than obvious "pollution." The causal chain of the deterioration is easily followed to its source. Too many cars, too many factories, too much detergent, too much pesticide, multiplying contrails, inadequate sewage treatment plants, too little water, too much carbon dioxide—all can be traced easily to too many people.

Of course, a smaller population could eventually destroy the ability of the planet to support sizable numbers of human beings. This could occur through the profligate use of weapons as diverse as chlorinated hydrocarbon insecticides or thermonuclear bombs. But with a human population of, say, one-half billion people, some minor changes in technology and some major changes in the rate of use and equity of distribution of the world's resources, there would clearly be no environmental crisis. Equally, regardless of changes in technology or resource consumption and distribution, current rates of population growth guarantee an environmental crisis which will persist until the final collapse.[32]

Chapter 2
THE ENDS OF THE ROAD

Too many people—that is why we are on the verge of the "death rate solution." Let's look briefly at what form that solution might take. The agencies most likely to result in a drastic rise in the death rate in the next few decades are exactly those most actively operating in pre-explosion human populations. They are three of the four apocalyptic horsemen—war, pestilence, and famine. Rapid improvement in public health, advances in agriculture, and improved transport systems have temporarily reduced the efficacy of pestilence and famine as population regulators. Improved technology has, on the other hand, greatly increased the potential of war as a population control device. Indeed, it has given us the means for self-extermination.

It now seems inevitable that death through starvation will be at least one factor in the coming increase in the death rate. If we succeed in avoiding plague or war, it may be the major factor. It is all too easy, however, for a layman to discount the potential for population control possessed today by plague. It is true that medical science has made tremendous advances against communicable diseases, but that does not mean that these diseases may now be ignored. As population density increases, so does the per capita shortage of medical personnel, so do problems of sanitation, and so do populations of disease-harboring organisms such as rats. In addition, malnutrition makes people weaker and more susceptible to infection. With these changes and with people living cheek by jowl, some of mankind's old enemies, like bubonic plague and cholera, may once again be on the move. As hunger and poverty increase, the resources that nations put into the control of vectors (disease-spreading organisms) may be reduced. Malaria, yellow fever, typhus, and their friends are still around—indeed, malaria is still a major killer and disabler of man. These ancient enemies of *Homo sapiens* are just waiting for the resurgence of mosquitoes, lice, and other vectors, to ride high again.

Viruses present an additional possibility. For reasons that are not entirely understood, virus diseases vary in their seriousness. For instance, viruses may become more potent as they circulate in large populations. It is not inconceivable that we will, one of these days, have a visitation from a "super flu," perhaps much more virulent than the famous killer of 1918–1920. That global epidemic killed some 25 million people. A proportionate mortality in the double 1918 population of the near future would be 50 million people, although modern antibiotics might prevent secondary bacterial infections which presumably killed many in 1918–1920. But what if a much more lethal strain should get going in the starving, more crowded population of a few years from now? This could happen naturally or through the escape of a special strain created for biological warfare. Modern transport systems would guarantee its rapid invasion of the far corners of the globe. It would be impossible for vaccines to be produced and distributed in time to affect the course of the epidemic in most areas. A great strain would be placed on facilities for production and distribution of antibiotics. Incapacitation of people in vital transport and agricultural occupations would add to the horror by worsening famine in many areas. A net result of 1.2 billion deaths—one out of every three people—is not inconceivable. By comparison, during World War II only about one out of 200 human beings then alive died in battle.

We came close to disaster in 1967. A virus disease, never seen before in human beings, transferred from a colony of vervet monkeys to research workers in laboratories in Marburg, Germany, and in Yugoslavia. Of the 32 people who contracted it, seven died, in spite of excellent medical care and the fact that they were all healthy adults. Two weeks before the disease, named Marburgvirus, broke out in the laboratories, the monkeys had been in London Airport. If the disease had appeared then, it could have spread throughout the world literally within hours.

Thermonuclear war could also provide a death rate solution to our problems, if it did not end them altogether by rendering *Homo sapiens* extinct. Politicians and war-games specialists like to postulate recovery programs following such a war, based on different numbers of survivors. However, several very critical factors are omitted from their calculations. Among these is the impact upon the environment of a nuclear exchange. These planners seem to think that survivors would emerge from their shelters, rebuild the cities, and go on as if nothing had happened. But it wouldn't be that simple. Even "clean" nuclear war over the North American continent would burn off vast areas of vegetation in huge fire-storms. This would doubtless produce violent weather changes and unprotected topsoil would be washed into the sea. The silt would have adverse effects on fisheries around our shores, as would oil and other materials flowing into the sea from our ruined civilization. Thus both farmland and fisheries would be damaged at a stroke.

Postwar planners also do not consider the psychological aftermath of such a holocaust. The virtually demolished "post-attack" world would be demoralizing, to say the least. If the physical paraphernalia of industry were destroyed and not quickly restored, industrial civilization would probably permanently disappear, even if large numbers of people survived. The resources are no longer available to start the industrial revolution over again. High-grade iron, copper, and other ores are no longer easily accessible; nor does oil bubble to the surface. Industrial technology itself is essential in order to keep industry going.

Obviously, we cannot discuss all of the possible courses of events as the world crisis deepens. It seems inevitable that world political tensions will increase as the disparity between "haves" and "have-nots" increases and as the penalties of being in a "have-not" nation become more and more severe. The chances of war increase with each addition to the population, intensifying competition for dwindling resources and food. Political events will have powerful influences on exactly how the death rate increases. They will affect how much food is grown and how it is distributed. They will affect the possibilities of plague. They will affect birth rates, especially in ODCs. They will affect the chances of effective international action. The possibilities are infinite; the single course of events that will be realized is unguessable. We can, however, look at a few possibilities, using a device known as a "scenario." Scenarios are hypothetical sequences of events used as an aid in thinking about the future, especially in identifying possible decision points. I'd like to offer three scenarios, giving three possible projections of what the next fifteen years or so could be like. One is in the form of a short story, one a sequence of hypothetical news items, and one a condensed history written in the future.

Remember, these are just possibilities, not predictions. We can be sure that none of them will come true exactly as stated, but they describe the kinds of events that might occur in the next few decades.

Scenario I

President Burrell was bored with the meteorology briefing. What did he care about the albedo, the properties of ice crystals, the greenhouse effect? The 1984 elections were on his mind—how the hell could he get reelected if he were responsible for instituting the first food rationing since World War II? The answer, he knew very well, was that he couldn't, and reelection was all that he really cared about. He put down his coffee cup and spoke to the intense young man standing at the blackboard.

"Let's get to the point, Dr. Moss. Will we or won't we be able to get a decent wheat crop this year?"

Moss threw his chalk onto the ledge below the board. "You know I can't give you any guaranteed predictions. Last year was a disaster—less than 30 million metric tons harvested. The chances are that this year will be much worse. We'll be lucky to get in 25 million. The weather isn't the only variable. A lot depends on the success of the new wheat-stem sawfly program. But my guess is that the wheat will follow much the same pattern as corn—a few years of decline, followed by a precipitous crash when many farmers simply refuse to plant any more."

The President turned to his Advisor in Biology. "What do you have to say, Professor Gilsinger?"

Gilsinger hesitated and then replied rapidly.

"I can't speak with certainty either, Mr. President. The National Academy Committee Report shows that we're clearly in a double bind. Considering the steady decline of the oceanic fisheries, we don't dare use massive doses of chlorinated hydrocarbons, and this damn bug is highly resistant to them anyway. We could use massive treatment with neo-parathion but it would be expensive and dangerous. Furthermore, it would be a serious setback to our efforts to establish rational controls, and we can't guarantee it would be successful for more than a couple of seasons."

"Les, what do you say?" Burrell asked his Secretary of Agriculture.

"I say I want to resign, Charlie. My hide won't be worth two cents in the wheat belt if we don't let them at least try the new methoxychlor derivative. The farmers there couldn't care less about the fisheries—they're fighting for their lives. And you wouldn't get one goddamn vote in those states in 1984."

Burrell wished for a moment his old friend from Kansas wasn't so quick and so right. "What if we subsidize a neo-parathion blitz?"

Lester Jones looked grim. "We'll be held responsible for the inevitable deaths—neo-parathion is nasty stuff. The crop will probably fail because of the weather, but they'll blame us for not letting them use methoxychlor-D."

Gilsinger cut in. "Mr. President, *I'll* have to resign if you do that; my colleagues would lynch me! Half of the Environmental Protection Agency will quit, too. And if you're going to make that decision, Mr. Tate had better be informed."

Burrell knew he was right. Bud Tate would blow his stack. The Secretary of State had led the U.N. battle to achieve a total international ban on chlorinated hydrocarbon insecticides—a ban ratified by all major nations in 1982, one short year before. If the U. S. went back on it, there would be hell to pay. The nations whose lives depended on high fisheries yields were hanging on the ropes. The decline which had started in 1969 had accelerated all too quickly. He thought with alarm, it could even mean a war with Japan. The development of a nuclear capability by starvation-wracked Japan was never far from his mind.

* * *

Jane Gilsinger was not worried about anybody's nuclear capability. Like most American housewives in 1983, she was preoccupied with how to feed her family adequately and safely. George made a good living; the university still carried him on the payroll at half-salary, and his government stipend more than made up the difference. Still, at a cost of $12 a pound, steak had become a memory for them as for most other Americans. She didn't really understand what the failure of the corn crop had to do with beef prices—but apparently it was a lot.

Tonight, though, she was happy. By getting to the supermarket early she had been able to get some of the special low-mercury cod for dinner—cod that, in addition, tested out at less than 22 ppm total chlorinates. George would insist that it be fed only to the children, as he always did whenever she was lucky enough to find low-residue seafoods, but he would be pleased.

However, George was more depressed than she had ever seen him when he reached home. He scarcely reacted to the news about the cod. With care born of long experience, Jane probed him about his day. He sighed and looked even more dejected. "You might as well know—it will be in the morning papers. The Council met this afternoon; the President has decided to institute food rationing. It's going to be very strict from the start."

"But that should make you happy. You've been

recommending it long enough. You've said all along that even tightening up the population control program couldn't possibly produce results fast enough to avoid this."

"No, of course it can't! Even with rationing, a lot of Americans are going to starve to death unless this climate change reverses. We've seen the trends clearly since the early 1970s, but nobody believed it would happen here, even after the 1976 Latin American famine and the Indian Dissolution. Almost a billion human beings starved to death in the last decade, and we managed to keep the lid on by a combination of good luck and brute force."

"I still don't understand—why are you so depressed when the President's finally taking your advice?"

"The stupid bastard is going to authorize the use of methoxychlor-D to try to save the wheat crop. He says he's got to have the wheat belt votes, especially now that he's been forced into rationing. I've resigned. Button and Willoby have, too. It's back to Pasadena for us."

Pasadena. Jane shuddered at the thought. The Washington area was bad enough. The ghetto riots which had erupted when the Family-Size Regulation Act had been passed had not reached them in Bethesda, but life since then had been tense, to say the least. But Pasadena! Cal Tech was no longer a pleasant place to work, and Pasadena had never, in her experience, been a pleasant place to live. She could always picture what the smog was doing to Peter and Julia's lungs. She didn't want to go back to carrying a purse full of quarters for the "Breath-a-life" machines. Although the machines had appeared around Washington in the last few years, the one minute of oxygen they supplied was not yet a matter of life and death. Pasadena was another story.

"George," she said hopefully, "do you suppose the Distinguished Professorship they offered you at Kansas would still be open?"

"I tried to call them this afternoon—I'm not looking forward to going back to Pasadena any more than you are, and the smog at Lawrence isn't even as bad as here. But Ma Bell's system was out again and I never got through." He didn't add that if Bud Tate was right about the impact of the methoxychlor-D decision on the deteriorating international situation, the lower levels of smog would be just one advantage of living in Kansas. No use frightening her unnecessarily, but choosing the University of Kansas in preference to Cal Tech would be easy under the circumstances.

* * *

Margaret Andrews had had very few choices in her life since Richard had been killed in the riots. He had died because of the things she had loved him for; his refusal to knuckle under to the dominant white society and, especially, his feeling of community with the oppressed people of the Third World. The callousness of American decisions during the great famine had all but driven him mad. The clarity with which the Population Control Law was aimed at the blacks and the poor had been the last straw. Even though they had carefully planned their two children, Richard had refused to speak out against the cries of revolution in the ghetto high school where he taught history. His patience was at an end, and his life soon ended also, snuffed out by a random bullet fired in the worst civil disorder in the history of the United States.

Margaret had struggled on for the sake of her children, overcoming her own lack of interest in life. But with 27% of the population out of work, there were no jobs for black women with degrees in English literature. Welfare was the only answer, and welfare wasn't enough. Young Richard outlived his father by less than a year. The death certificate said pneumonia, but she knew it was malnutrition. Now surveying the crumbling one-room flat which she shared with Janet Brown, she came to her decision.

"Janet," she said softly. Her dozing friend started and opened her eyes. "I'm leaving. I'm taking Freddy south."

"What in heaven's name for?" In spite of her just completed eight-hour shift as a supermarket clerk, Janet was now wide awake.

"Haven't you heard the news about the rationing? The amount of food allowable on the stamps will be cut by at least one-third."

"My God, we're losing ground on what we can get now. The soy cakes are more expensive every day. And that so-called bread! . . ."

"Exactly. I won't stay here and watch Freddy go the same way Junior did. My mother still has a piece of land in Alabama. Maybe we can grow enough to live on."

*   *   *

President Burrell glared at his Secretary of State. "Goddamn it, Bud, I don't care what Smersky says. He isn't facing an election next year. Surely the Russians aren't going to risk an all-out war over a lousy pesticide! Tell them it's a matter of life and death for us."

"They think it's a matter of life and death for *them*. What's worse, for the first time this century the Japanese and Chinese are standing shoulder-to-shoulder with the Soviets, and all the nations of Western Europe may join them. Even Australia and New Zealand have protested. We'll be massacred at the U.N. Charley, those people are deadly serious."

"I just can't buy that. You're letting your personal role in negotiating the ban influence your judgment. I know my action is an embarrassment to you, Bud," the President's tone was now conciliatory. "But it's for the good of the country."

Tate was in no mood to be placated. "The good of the

party and its leader, don't you mean?" he snapped. "The country will hardly benefit from a thermonuclear war!"

"My decision stands. The Joint Chiefs assure me that the Japanese-Sino-Soviet axis is all bluff. The Japanese would just love to get those Siberian resources all for themselves, and so would Kai Chen. The Russians know they can't trust the orientals in a real showdown."

Tate would not back down. "Why the phase two alert, if everything is so cut and dried?"

"Just standard precautions. Now go back to the U.N. and give them the 'extraordinary threat to our national existence' line. They'll have to buy it."

Tate shook his head. "I'm sorry, Charley, I can't."

"Bud, I can't work with people who won't go along with my decisions once they're made; you're an old friend, but . . ."

"Don't worry, Mr. President," Tate replied stiffly. "You'll have my resignation within the hour. Leo Kramer is thoroughly briefed and can carry the ball until you decide on a new secretary."

* * *

Relieved as she was with the good news about the Kansas professorship, Jane could not suppress her apprehensions. The U.N. action had been unprecedented— a total embargo on all commerce with the United States and $100 million per day reparations to WHO for every day the methoxychlor-D program continued. George's arm around Jane as they listened to President Burrell's address on the TV did little to reassure her. Neither did the President's words. He was obviously in over his head.

"And, my fellow Americans, it is just as well that the great Communist conspiracy has shown its true colors at this turning point in history. I cannot believe that democratic Japan and other nations historically friendly to us will attempt to implement the rash action they so hastily approved at the United Nations. Our resolve is being tested—we shall be equal to the test."

"He still doesn't get it," George said as he switched off the set. "The poor slob still thinks politics and economics are more important than ecology. I think we'd better pack immediately; he's not going to back down."

"Do you think we'll be attacked?" Jane could hardly believe it was all happening. Her entire life had been lived under the shadow of "the bomb." That it would ever actually be used again was almost beyond imagining.

"I doubt it, dear, but I think we may attack them. The idea of preventive war has been popular with our military for decades. Burrell's just the boy to turn them loose."

* * *

Margaret Andrews was in tears when her mother greeted her at the door of the run-down farmhouse. Traveling must have been better during segregation—even the privation of black Washington was nothing compared to the hunger and abuse she and Freddy had faced on the road. It was after dinner before she could bring herself to talk about it.

"Mom, it was just awful. We didn't have any ration cards because they weren't issued until after we'd left. We managed to buy a little food in a store in Virginia—some three-day old bread and some awful sausage, but that's all we had for four days. I wasted almost a day in Charlotte trying to get ration cards but the man there claimed they could only be issued to residents. When I tried to argue he called a cop. And when the cop saw the 'welfare' stamp on my I.D. he gave me an hour to get out of town. Freddy was crying, he was so hungry, and this big white cop told me to shut him up or he would!"

"It's O.K. now, honey—you're home."

* * *

Burrell was very nervous as he strapped himself into the rear seat of the VTOL jet fighter poised on the south lawn of the White House. The preemptive strike was a momentous and frightening decision—and now there was the chance the United States would be beaten to the draw.

"I'm ready, Major Levy." He spoke into the microphone in his helmet as the air force sergeant who had strapped him in dropped back to the ground. "But I don't see why this damn thing was necessary. I should have taken the helicopter to the war center."

"Too slow, sir," the pilot replied, his hands flying through the start procedure. "Our orders are to get you out fast. Hold on."

The small group on the lawn covered their ears as the twin turbines fired up and the curiously conventional-looking fighter rose gracefully from the lawn and then accelerated rapidly toward the southwest. Two pairs of F-111s which had been orbiting above cranked their wings back and took up positions above and behind. Burrell contemplated the seeming peace of the smog-shrouded countryside as the five jets streaked along at 20,000 feet.

Even higher, above the stratosphere, another vehicle streaked toward the same target. Its covering was a special compound, designed to minimize radar returns. The vehicle periodically ejected small capsules cleverly engineered to produce a specific radar image as they hurtled through the outer atmosphere. As each one plunged into thicker air, it began to glow and then produce its own fiery shroud. But clever discrimination techniques prevailed, and the vehicle with the payload was identified. The warhead could not see or avoid the ultra-fast missile which sprang at it from the rolling hills of Appalachia.

The flash of the exploding "Sprint" warhead bathed Burrell's plane with a light that dispelled the gathering twilight. He looked up as the pilot shouted "Hang on!" The blast wave slammed them downward and to the right. Burrell's head snapped back as the fighter accelerated into a steep spiral dive. Major Levy stopped the turn and hauled back on the yoke as the airspeed indicator moved rapidly to and beyond the red line. His last thought was to hope that the structure would hold as he was bound to pull more g's in the recovery than the bird was stressed for. He need not have worried. As he began his recovery, one of the F-111s, minus a wing, spun into his fighter. Neither the pilot nor Burrell even lived to see the northern horizon transformed into a solid mass of flame.

*   *   *

The Gilsingers could hardly believe that warm weather had come at last. The stubble in the field behind their ancient stone farmhouse at last was free of snow—and the 21st of June was only a week away. George hobbled to the window; his leg, wounded in the last attack on the farmhouse two months before, had not completely healed. He peered out between the boards.

"Jane, we've got to get our garden going right away. We're getting weak on the short rations and so are Ken and Sue. What's worse, we won't be able to feed the kids full rations much longer."

"I know," she replied. "I can hardly bear the thought of moving. And we'll be so exposed outside. What if some of those hooligans come out from Kansas City?"

"I think they must all be dead from starvation or radiation poisoning. Thank God this old place wasn't burned by Quantrill, or we would have been too. A foot of stone stops more than bullets. Here comes Ken."

Ken Barnard, Professor of Physics at the now-defunct University of Kansas, moved slowly across the field, his twelve-gauge shotgun held alertly as if he were on an infantry patrol. Jane moved to the door and opened the heavy bolts.

"What a mess!" Ken burst out as he moved into the room and sank onto the battered couch. "It's almost as if Quantrill had done it again 130 years later and sowed salt on the ruins—much worse than last fall. Any survivors have cleared off." He rose from the couch. "I'd better get out of these clothes quickly; the radiation level is still pretty high."

"Any food?" Jane looked hopeful.

"Two tins of pears—of all the lousy luck. The looting has been thorough. How's Sue?"

"Still the same. And I'm afraid that Julia's radiation sickness is getting worse."

George quickly changed the subject. "Do you think it will be safe to plant our seeds?"

Ken nodded. "Yeah. If there are any other people alive in Kansas, I don't think they'll find us. But I moved what's left of those last two onto the road and drove stakes through them as a warning—just in case."

"I'll go look at Sue." Jane wearily headed for the other room.

"Now that she's gone, I'll tell you the truth." Ken moved over to where George was standing, still staring out of the window. "We can probably grow some food, but without clearing at least a foot of topsoil it won't be edible. And without the topsoil I don't know what we'll grow."

"Counts still that high?"

"I warned you they would be. My guess is that the exposure we'll get doing the clearing, planting, and harvesting has about a 95% chance of being fatal. If the radioactivity level of the rain stayed at even 50% of its present level the food wouldn't be edible anyway."

"I guessed as much." George shook his head. "And unless I'm wrong, the growing season will be lousy anyway. The cooling effect was obviously beyond the worst DOD projections—too much crap injected into the stratosphere."

"I think we've probably started an ice age spiral, but it won't make much difference to us."

"I suppose we might as well give it a try. No use letting the girls know before we have to."

"Right. We're lucky in one way, though."

"What's that?"

"We might not have had easy access to the cyanide before the attack. Now we've got more than enough when the time comes."

*   *   *

Freddy was happy behind the plow. The mule was strong, and the work was going well. Only in some parts of the southeast had survival been possible and he'd been one of the lucky ones. His mother had died after a twenty-year battle with radiation-induced illness; but they'd had some good times, and she'd lived to see him marry Louise. If only she'd lived to see the baby born and known that it was all right. So few were.

The lump in his armpit bothered him more now, as he wrestled with the plow. Although he was uneducated, he knew its significance. But he was lucky. He and Louise had a baby, and the baby had a chance. What more could a man ask?

Scenario II

The first three news stories in this scenario are genuine; the rest are based upon them. A similar scenario could have been constructed around the 1967 Marburg-virus incident.

NEW FEVER VIRUS SO DEADLY THAT RESEARCH HALTS, by Lawrence K. Altman (*New York Times,* February 10, 1970).

American doctors have discovered a virus so virulent that they have stopped their research into its mysteries.

The virus, called Lassa fever, killed three of the five Americans it infected during the last year . . .

Lassa fever infection can involve almost all the body's organs. The virus produces a fever as high as 107 degrees, mouth ulcers, a skin rash with tiny hemorrhages, pnuemonia, infection of the heart leading to cardiac failure, kidney damage, and severe muscle aches.

Dr. Jordi Casals . . . and his coworker, Dr. Sonja Buckley . . . named it for the place from which it came, which was Lassa, a village of about 1,000 Nigerians, situated about 150 miles below the Sahara . . .

SPREAD OF DEADLY VIRAL FEVER IS SUSPECTED IN NIGERIA, by Lawrence K. Altman (*New York Times,* February 18, 1970).

The American scientists who discovered the virus that causes Lassa fever suspect that there is now an outbreak of the lethal disease in Jos, a tin-mining town in northern Nigeria.

Ten of 20 Nigerian and American patients died at Evangel Hospital in Jos of what is suspected to be Lassa fever in recent weeks . . .

Because of their experience with Lassa fever a year ago, doctors at Jos suspected the disease when the 20 patients became ill recently. They, too, had a high fatality rate—50 percent . . .

The greatest mystery is where the disease came from. Doctors suspect it was transmitted originally from an animal—which one they do not know—but that the patients with known Lassa fever acquired the infection from each other.

Of more than curiosity now is the fact that last year's cases and this year's outbreak have occurred during the same months—January and February . . .

THREAT TO NIGERIA FROM LASSA FEVER FOUND TO BE OVER. Lagos (Associated Press, March 14, 1970).

Doctors studying Lassa fever, a mystifying virus that has proved very dangerous to work on, say the disease no longer threatens the northern Nigeria area where it was discovered . . .

LASSA FEVER AGAIN IN NIGERIA. Lagos (United Press, February 12, 1973).

Fifteen people in Nigeria have come down with what is believed to be Lassa fever . . . Three have died so far this year in Jos and two others from neighboring villages . . . Doctors at the University of Ibadan are working to develop a plasma serum from the blood of an early survivor in an effort to save the eight who are still critically ill . . .

NEW DISEASE REPORTED IN GHANA. Accra (Reuters, March 5, 1973).

An unknown virus disease has stricken the village of Lmuto, 50 miles from Accra. Seven people have died in the last week. The village has been strictly quarantined and no new cases have appeared since last Tuesday . . .

LASSA FEVER CONTAINED. Lagos (United Press, March 17, 1973).

Last month's outbreak of Lassa fever in Nigeria is now believed controlled, local medical authorities say. There have been no new cases since March 2 . . . In total, 27 people are believed to have been infected. Sixteen survived, in part thanks to prompt action by doctors at the University of Ibadan, whose serum was developed in time to save at least five of the survivors . . .

Research is proceeding in Ibadan and in Atlanta, Georgia, to develop a more effective way of combating the dangerous virus . . .

EPIDEMIC IN MOZAMBIQUE. Tete (Reuters, August 23, 1973).

Reports from missionary medical stations in remote areas south and west of Tete indicate that some unknown disease is assuming epidemic proportions. At least 130 people have died from it. The disease does not respond either to sulfa or to antibiotic drugs . . .

DISEASE IN TANZANIA. Dar es Salaam (United Press, September 6, 1973).

A mysterious virus disease that appeared in Mozambique last month has been reported in southern Tanzania . . . The borders between the two countries have been temporarily closed . . .

VIRUS ESCAPES IN ATLANTA. Atlanta, Ga. (Associated Press, November 13, 1973).

Three technicians and a virologist have been diagnosed as having Lassa fever . . . Two of the technicians were involved in research on the virus. The other is not known to have been in contact with the disease . . .

NEW CASES IN GEORGIA. Atlanta, Ga. (Associated Press, December 6, 1973).

Lassa fever has appeared in Athens, Georgia, where six people have contracted it . . . Two technicians in Atlanta have died, the others are recuperating. Serum is being developed from their blood plasma. But so much plasma is needed for each new patient, there is little hope of curing all six . . .

No progress has been reported in the development of a vaccine either at the virus center in Nigeria, where the disease was first diagnosed . . .

AFRICAN DISEASE IN INDIA. Bombay (Reuters, December 18, 1973).

A mysterious virus disease, probably one which is now epidemic in Mozambique and southern Tanzania, has broken out in Bombay. Doctors believe that it was brought by Indian residents of Tanzania who came to Bombay . . .

INDIAN DISEASE MAY BE LASSA FEVER. New Delhi (Associated Press, January 4, 1974).

Doctors at the University of Delhi believe that the unknown virus disease that is overrunning India may be Lassa fever . . . Tests are now being conducted . . .

New cases are being reported daily in Calcutta, Bombay, and Delhi . . . Deaths seem to be running at a rate of 60 to 70% . . .

Tanzania and Mozambique both report failure in

containing the disease. Cases have now been reported in Zambia, Kenya, and Rhodesia . . .

The escaped virus in the United States seems to have been suppressed, after nine deaths and 21 reported cases in the state of Georgia . . .

INDIAN DEATH TOLL REACHES 5,000 (United Press, January 6, 1974).

Known deaths in India from Lassa fever are 5,038 and cases are being reported from new states . . .

Deaths in Africa are estimated to be as high as 7,000 by some authorities . . . Squatters have begun leaving such cities as Dar es Salaam and Nairobi . . . Quarantines have proved ineffective in controlling the spread of the virus . . . Cases have appeared in West Africa and Egypt . . .

LASSA FEVER IN EUROPE. Rome (Reuters, January 8, 1974).

Isolated cases of what may be Lassa fever have appeared in two port cities in Italy and one in Greece . . .

NEW CASES IN U. S. New York (United Press, January 9, 1974).

Lassa fever has broken out again in three southern states, Georgia, South Carolina, and Tennessee . . . Three more deaths have occurred since the earlier escape from an Atlanta laboratory . . . Incorrect diagnosis in rural clinics is believed to have contributed to the notion that the disease had been contained . . .

LASSA FEVER CALLED PANDEMIC (*New York Times,* January 13, 1974).

Lassa fever has now appeared on all major continents except Australia. It was reported in Brazil and Chile yesterday. New cases have been at least tentatively identified in Odessa, USSR, most Mediterranean countries,

England, France, Germany, Austria, Mexico, Turkey, Morocco, all of Africa south of the Sahara. The disease is believed to be widespread in parts of Southeast Asia, but the turmoil caused by the war there makes certain identification difficult . . . China has not admitted having Lassa fever, but authorities feel that it will soon spread there if it has not already . . .

AUSTRALIA AND NEW ZEALAND CLOSE BORDERS (*New York Times,* January 15, 1974).

Prime Minister Gorton of Australia today announced that Australia's borders will be closed until the Lassa fever pandemic has run its course or has been halted through medical means. New Zealand's government has made a similar announcement . . . Only essential importation will be permitted, after suitable quarantine measures for delivery have been set up.

Medical authorities have reported no success in developing a vaccine for Lassa fever or in discovering the means of transmission . . .

India has declared a national emergency . . . Medical stations have been established in towns and villages to treat the sick. The death toll has passed 10,000. The disease is fatal in about 70% of diagnosed cases. It spreads fastest and death rates are highest among the crowded and malnourished poor there as in other countries . . .

A U.N. spokesman has said that a combination of a very large, dense, generally poverty-stricken and hungry world population with rapid intercontinental transportation systems are the basic causes for the severity of the pandemic and the speed with which it has spread.

The disease is believed to be rampant in at least two Chinese cities and adjacent rural areas . . . It now exists in every country in Asia and Africa . . .

CHINA ACCUSES USSR OF BW (*New York Times,* January 20, 1974).

Radio Peking, in its most vindictive broadcast in months, today accused the Soviet Union of practicing biological warfare . . .

The Lassa outbreak in the U.S. is reported out of control. The disease is apparently increasing among slum dwellers in large cities and the rural poor, especially in the South . . . The death rates in North America and Europe seem to be about 55%. As more plasma serum is developed and distributed, this percentage is expected to drop . . .

WORLD DEATH TOLL NEARS MILLION (Reuters, January 21, 1974).

The United Nations today announced that at the present rate of acceleration, deaths from Lassa fever would reach one million by January 22, and that three million cases will have appeared by the end of the week.

Most countries report considerable disruption of normal activities and states of emergency prevail in most cities . . . Refugees are fleeing metropolitan centers in Africa, Latin America, and India by the millions. Public transport and food distribution in cities around the world have been seriously hampered by absenteeism . . . Nonessential businesses in large U.S. and European cities have closed offices for the duration of the emergency . . . Volunteers are being mobilized to distribute food and keep power plants and transportation systems operating.

Medical authorities report that an effective vaccine is still months away. Crash research programs are going on in several countries. Plasma serum is still scarce in developed countries, but the disease death rate has dropped to 53%. Top priority for serum is given to medical personnel and children. Minorities in the U.S.

complain that serum is available only to "establishment patients" who can afford it . . .

Serum is generally unavailable in underdeveloped areas, and medical facilities have been swamped. U.N. agencies have been trying to distribute serum, but with little effect. Death rates range between 65 and 75%. It is rumored that black markets for serum have appeared in the Middle East, North Africa, and some Latin American countries . . .

EIGHT MILLION DEAD OF LASSA FEVER (*Washington Post,* February 8, 1974).

U.N. authorities now estimate that over 8 million victims have been claimed by Lassa fever, including 5 million in Asia. The disease continues to spread unchecked, except for quarantined Australia, New Zealand, and Hawaii . . .

The social system is breaking down in India. Food riots have been reported in Calcutta and Bombay and several smaller cities. The dead are now being buried in mass graves . . .

There is little news from Africa, but it is believed that conditions in most sub-Sahara countries except South Africa are nearly as bad as in India . . .

The long recovery period of survivors is believed responsible for much of the social disruption . . .

AUSTRALIA GETS L.F. (United Press, February 12, 1974).

A Sydney dock worker today came down with what is believed to be Lassa fever. Serum is being flown from the U.S. to treat him. The dock worker and medical personnel tending him are being kept in strict isolation . . .

The quarantine regulations regarding foreign trade have been further tightened to prevent more occurrences . . .

30 MILLION DEAD *(New York Times,* February 19, 1974).

U.N. sources say that the number of cases of Lassa fever is doubling about every week . . .

Agricultural leaders have expressed concern that spring planting of crops in the Northern Hemisphere can be carried out. Some countries are establishing volunteer programs utilizing urban workers in non-essential industries . . .

CHINA ADMITS NO BW *(The Australian,* February 23, 1974).

Radio Peking reversed its previous belligerent stand today and proposed a plan for international cooperation between China, the USSR, Europe, and the U.S. in finding a cure for Lassa fever as rapidly as possible. China is estimated to have had more than 6 million deaths from Lassa fever . . . Hong King reports a massive influx of refugees in the last week. These refugees describe scenes of mass disruption and chaos in China . . .

Nearly 1.5 million have died in the U.S., 4 million in Europe . . . Bread lines and government food distribution centers have been established in all countries . . . Mass migration from cities has been reported . . .

Australia is still free of Lassa fever. The Sydney dock worker is still the only case here. He is reported out of danger . . .

A University of Sydney virologist has speculated that even if Lassa fever should gain a foothold in Australia, it would be relatively easy to contain it or to delay its spread. This is because Australia is so sparsely populated outside her cities. An infected city could be quarantined from the others.

Because of rampant Lassa fever, the war in Southeast Asia is virtually at a standstill . . .

DISEASE CLAIMS 120 MILLION (*New York Times,* March 3, 1974).

. . . U.N. sources report that the incidence of the disease is no longer accelerating quite so fast as a few weeks ago, although the absolute numbers of sick and dead continue to rise astronomically. They project that the ultimate death toll may be well over one billion, assuming no significant change in lethality of the virus. This might be mitigated by the perfection of an effective vaccine. The disease is expected to run its course in four to six more weeks at the present rate of spread.

The serum situation is slowly improving, but even in developed countries only about one-quarter of the sick can be treated. In underdeveloped areas, the situation is worse . . .

Assessing the present world situation is becoming more difficult as wire services and radio news become more erratic . . .

Many deaths from starvation have been reported from areas of rural India and Brazil, where sickness has destroyed normal food distribution channels . . .

WORST IS OVER (*New York Times,* May 15, 1974).

The World Health Organization announced today that Lassa fever is definitely on the decline. There is now, for the first time, enough serum to treat all new cases . . .

An estimated 1.12 billion men, women, and children have perished from the disease. Another 300 to 400 million are believed to have died of other causes related to the pandemic, including starvation, other diseases, riots, and civil disorder. The ultimate toll may reach one and one-half billion, or one-third of the entire population of the world. The heaviest toll of course was among children and old people. It will take years, perhaps decades to recover . . .

LEADERS MEET AT U.N. (*New York Times*, June 2, 1974).

The assembled heads of state of 72 nations, including the U.S., China, the USSR, India, and most of Europe, together with delegates from the other nations represented in the U.N., yesterday passed a resolution designed to prevent events such as those of the past year from ever recurring. Stating that the lessons of overpopulation were clear for all to see, they unanimously voted complete cooperation in recovery measures, which were to be accompanied by strong population control, taking advantage of the reduced younger generation. The loss of nearly half the world's children was an immeasurably profound tragedy, they stated, and they offered the deepest sympathy to all bereaved parents (among whom were many of the leaders themselves). Nevertheless, the opportunity to establish population stability for the next two generations must be grasped.

A representative commission was authorized to make determinations of optimum populations for regions and for the world at a variety of standards of living, based on available resources and expected food production capability. In two years, June 1976, the world leaders would meet again to decide which possibility should be the long-term goal.

An Environmental Agency was also established to have control over all common features of the environment, including the oceans, the atmosphere, and international fresh waterways . . .

The hope was expressed that the U.N. might now develop into a genuinely powerful world regulatory body. As President Chai of the Security Council put it, "Men and nations have learned how dependent we all are upon one another and on the health of our little Spaceship Earth."

Scenario III

In 1978, it became obvious to the world that the food-population imbalance in much of Asia, Africa, and South America had reached the point of imminent catastrophe, despite increasingly generous assistance in agricultural development from the ODCs during the previous decade. The Green Revolution had succeeded in raising food production considerably for a few years but efforts to spread it to subsistence farmers in the poorest areas had failed. Increasing frequency and duration of local famines, and sudden declines in fishery catches, combined with progressive difficulties in maintaining the flow of "necessary" commodities toward the developed world, had driven the lesson home, especially to the United States. Dramatic changes in the world system in general and American foreign policy in particular were clearly required if a global disaster was to be avoided.

Action was taken in a remarkably short time. Despite internal disorders in many countries, which were causing difficulties in international trade, the U.S. government officially affirmed a new policy of total nonintervention, a policy it had informally been trying to pursue since the last forces had been withdrawn from Southeast Asia in 1973. The Agricultural Section of the Department of Natural Resources was instructed to purchase all food in storage beyond a one-year supply and make it available to the United Nations for distribution. Simultaneously, drastic restrictions were placed on imports of protein foods (fish, oilseeds, and nuts) from underdeveloped countries. To avoid loss of income to those poor nations, the United States guaranteed compensatory payments, the sole condition being that these foods be distributed to the hungry, rather than sold to other ODCs.

The American Ambassador to the United Nations, in what many people consider the most important political statement in human history, proposed an International Survival Tax on the overdeveloped nations to be paid to UDCs largely through the United Nations. It was proposed that it should be graduated according to each country's per capita income; below a per capita income of $500, a country would become a recipient. The Ambassador announced that the United States would begin paying an IST tax of 4% of its Gross National Product annually, some $45 billion in 1978, or double the amount expended for such assistance in 1977. One-half of the amount was assigned to the United Nations for disposal, the other half would be spent by the United States to run joint development programs in direct partnership with UDCs. The U.S. would again double its IST to 8% ($90 billion) by 1980. The Ambassador appealed to other ODCs to follow suit, and suggested that an immediate series of U.N. conferences be established to alter the world trade system to give a strong advantage to the UDCs.

Historians have long argued over what the decisive factors were in the general acceptance of the U.S. proposals by other ODCs. One group contends that it was the internal changes in the United States. The institution of food rationing and guarantees of equitable protein distribution among all Americans, the moral leadership of President Richards in openly condemning racist governors and congressmen, and the acceleration of the resource self-sufficiency and recycling programs were clearly important. So was the obvious determination on the part of most Americans to change the way they treated both their environment and their fellow human beings. As Gilbert Foster wrote in his classic *The Role of America in the Overdevelopment Crisis* (McGraw-Hill, New York, 2017): "In essence, the Spaceman Morality jelled almost overnight. The trends which had begun late in the 1960s culminated in a revolution of new ideals late in the 1970s."

More conventional historians, such as Sir Guy Selving, contend that the internal changes in the United States were unimportant compared with foreign policy changes in influencing the behavior of other nations. He points to the steady withdrawal of United States troops from overseas following the last crisis in Berlin and the Indochina war. That, in conjunction with U.S. support for the admission of the People's Republic of China into the United Nations and the 1976 assistance treaty with Cuba, indicated to the socialist nations of the world that America had lost interest in forcing its views and political system on the entire world. Simultaneously, grave internal difficulties in the Soviet Union, Poland, China, Cuba, and several other socialist nations had made it clear that planned economies were not exempt from the population-environment crisis that was racking the world.

Whichever school is correct, the cooperative action initiated in a few short months of 1978 forms the basis of today's World Commons Control System—the arrangement of international controls over population, resources, and the environment which all nations agree are moving us into a new era for humanity. In many ways it is a miracle that this cooperation survived the 1980s, a decade of dissolution. World action came too late for almost one billion people. In spite of massive attempts to increase food production, limit food loss between harvest and table, and achieve equitable distribution, a minimum of 70 million people died annually during the entire decade from starvation and starvation-related diseases. There was no net population growth between 1979 and 1991, despite only a slight decline in birth rates. The decade was marked by intense disorder in many UDCs, with occasional periods of violent uprising. It is certain that only the generosity and cooperative spirit of the people and governments of all ODCs prevented the situation from deteriorating into a global war. As Premier Yen-Chu of China said in his famous 1985 address to the U.N. General Assembly, "How can I speak of the United States and the Soviet Union as my enemies? Every day American naval supply vessels bring food and technicians into our ports, while Russian trucks are pouring across our borders with fertilizers and heavy equipment we need desperately. The People's Republic of China hopes never to close its borders again."

We are now reaping the major benefits of the population control policies which began to go into effect in the 1980s. Between 1980 and 2000, the world birth rate declined from 31 to 25 per thousand. Although the death rate declined again to around 15 during the 1990s, the growth rate stayed below 1.2%. Since 2000 the growth rate has declined further, and the population is expected to peak at about 6 billion around 2055, after which we can look forward to a slow decline. The initiative of the Swedes, Chinese, Indians, Pakistanis, and Indonesians played critical roles in reducing birth rates, but major credit must go to the dramatic appeals of Pope Pius XIII. The moral leadership of a revitalized Catholic church tipped the balance for population control in a way that secular persuasion could not. The other individual who must be singled out for mention is Susan Freiberg, the first woman president of the United States. Her continued warnings against taking short-term gains in food production at the cost of long-term ecological destruction are believed ultimately to have saved an estimated two billion lives. The decisions of the 1970s and 1980s were the most heart-rending mankind as a whole has ever been forced to make; their memory has infused our species with a determination that such dilemmas will never again have to be faced.

It is impossible in a textbook to give you an emotional grasp of the greatest convulsion ever undergone by human society. In your next library session, call for tapes LW301 and LW302 so that you can sample personally the flavor of those exciting and difficult times.

This last scenario has considerably more appeal than the others, even though it presumes the death by starvation of as many as a billion people. Unfortunately, it also involves a maturity of outlook and behavior in the United States that seems unlikely to develop in the near future. I will leave you to decide which scenario is more realistic, and I challenge you to create one more optimistic than the last. (I won't accept one that starts, "In early 1972 the first monster space ships from a planet of the star Alpha Centauri arrive bearing CARE packages . . .")

Chapter 3

WHAT IS BEING DONE

Family Planning and Other Failures

A ship has hit the rocks and is sinking. The passengers scream for help. Some jump overboard and are devoured by the circling sharks. A group of distinguished scientists is on board. One of their number suggests that they can help man the pumps. "Oh, no!" shout the others. "That might hurt the captain's feelings. Besides, pumping is not our business. It's outside our field of competence." You can guess what they do. They appoint a committee to study the problem, with subcommittees on marine engineering and navigation. They announce to the passengers that in two or three years the committee will produce a wonderful report which will be acceptable to the passengers, the captain, and the steamship line. Not so passive are the politicians. Some jump up to say that the passengers don't understand the political realities of the situation. Other more progressive politicians grab thimbles and start bailing, stopping every few seconds to accept praise for their valiant efforts.

That about sums up the situation on the population control front in the United States and in much of the rest of the world. People in positions of power have either ignored the problem or have recommended solutions that are inadequate in scope or proven failures. The Catholic Church sanctions only the rhythm method

78

of contraception. Unfortunately, people who practice this method of contraception are commonly called "parents." Even under the most carefully controlled conditions women using this technique run a 15% risk of pregnancy each year they use it. (With the Pill comparable rates are less than 1%.) Of course, under normal conditions, the failure rate is much higher, about 25%. In short, the rhythm method doesn't work—the irreverent description of it as "Vatican roulette" is, alas, accurate. As Vatican roulette is to family planning, so family planning is to population control. Family planning doesn't work either.

The inadequacy of family planning in the field of population control has been brilliantly outlined by Kingsley Davis in an article in the magazine *Science*.[33] He points out that, "The things that make family planning acceptable are the very things that make it ineffective for population control. By stressing the right of parents to have the number of children they want, it evades the basic question of population policy, which is how to give societies the number of children they need. By offering only the means of *couples* to control fertility, it neglects the means for societies to do so." Or, as Justin Blackwelder once said, " 'Family planning' means, among other things, that if we are going to multiply like rabbits, we should do it on purpose. One couple may plan to have three children; another couple may plan seven. In both cases they are a cause of the population problem—not a solution to it." Above all, remember that planned, well-spaced children will starve, or vaporize in a thermonuclear war, or die of plague just as well as unplanned children.

The story is depressingly the same everywhere—people want large families. They want families of a size that will keep the population growing. If each couple had an average of just over two children (to replace themselves, with slight allowances for child mortality), population

growth would eventually stop after about two generations, and the population would stabilize. If the average
family had less than two children, growth could be
halted somewhat sooner, and a slow decline would set in.
However, far from wanting two or less children, people
in ODCs usually want from 2.5 to 3.5 children per
family, while in UDCs from 4 to 6 are considered ideal.
During the 1960s, surveys indicated that the average
desired family size for Americans was about 3.3 children. "Family planning," particularly in UDCs, is all too
often used to lock the barn door after the horse is stolen.
Davis reports that among 5,196 women seeking assistance in rural Punjab, India, two-thirds were over 30.
Since many were married before they were 15, it is
hardly surprising that more than half of them already
had six or more children. Similarly, the president of the
Hong Kong Family Planning Association pointed out
that, at least in the early years of their program, "the
patients who received assistance were usually about
thirty-one years of age and had six children." It is important to remember that, even if all women had exactly the
number of children they wanted, the results would still
be demographic catastrophe. Family planning is important from the point of view of the health and welfare of
individuals, but it does not control populations.

Current birth control programs in the UDCs have
their base in "family planning." Their goals are expressed, in almost all cases, in lowered birth rates.
Pakistan aimed to reduce its birth rate from 50 to 40
per thousand between 1960 and 1970. India aims to
reduce its birth rate from 40 to 25 "as soon as possible."
In 1970 Pakistan's birth rate was still 50 and India's
was 42. But remember, the critical thing is the *balance*
between birth and death rates. With death rates around
10 to 20, it is clear that even achieving these goals could
not, by any stretch of the imagination, be called "population control." People would still be multiplying like

rabbits and populations doubling every 30 to 40 years.

Let's take a look at family planning in India—a country whose government has been more than a decade ahead of ours in *recognizing* that population size is a matter for governmental concern and action. The Indian government has had an official birth control program since 1951. In the early years of their program they did a lot of experimenting with the rhythm method—although millions of Catholic couples could have given them the word on its efficiency. But recently they've gotten down to business. When I was in Delhi in 1966, posters that said, "Use loop for family planning," were much in evidence. The "loops," of course, refers to several different kinds of plastic devices which, inserted in the womb, prevent conception. These intrauterine devices (IUDs) are one of the main tools of family planning in India. Others are the simple and harmless male sterilization operation, the vasectomy, and the distribution of rubber sheaths (condoms).

In early 1968 Joseph Lelyveld [34] reported that only a small number of India's 335 districts had on hand a complete task force for birth control. One of these few districts is Kaira, an area in which each village has assigned to it a family planning worker. But after having active family planning workers in the district for eight years, its birth rate was still higher than the national average. Lelyveld told of the high hopes with which the IUD was greeted as a panacea for India's family planning problems—it was cheap, easily administered, and relatively permanent. But the high hopes were not realized. Although there was an initial spurt of enthusiasm, soon the number of insertions dropped to virtually zero. A principal reason was a series of rumors, some of which were alleged to have been spread by the Bombay office of an American drug company interested in pushing the Pill. The loop was supposed to stick copulating couples together. It was supposed to swim through the bloodstream to the brain. It was supposed to cause excess menstrual bleeding. It was supposed to cause cancer. It was supposed to give the man a shock during intercourse. Small wonder women shied away!

Efforts have been made to squelch the rumors, with some success. Unfortunately, the IUDs do cause increased menstrual bleeding in a small proportion of women, which made squelching rumors more difficult. In addition, malnourished women are more likely to have excess bleeding than are well-fed women. Thus malnourishment, a result of overpopulation, helps to prevent effective population control! In some areas the loop is again playing a role, but in the Kaira district it is not.

More recently I have heard the disturbing rumor that in some areas of India women are removing the IUDs so that they can collect again the small payment for having it inserted. Clearly, India has a long way to go with the IUDs.

What about vasectomies? A few years ago, there was talk in India of compulsory sterilization for all males who were fathers of three or more children. Ignore for a moment the socio-political problems that would be raised by such a program. Consider just the logistic problems, as A. S. Parkes did.[35] Even if those eligible could be rounded up, it would take 1,000 surgeons or para-surgeons operating eight hours a day, five days a week, a full eight years to sterilize the candidates who exist today. And the stock of candidates is growing very rapidly. Can you picture the probable results of a government attempt to sterilize 40 million American males? What a problem it would be in our country, with its relatively informed populace and efficient transport and communications system! Imagine such an attempt in India, where the difference between castration and sterilization (still not clear to many Westerners) would be almost impossible to explain. As one might expect, the principal Indian official thinking in such tough-minded terms, Dr. S. Chandrasekhar, ended up in a less influential position in a government shuffle.

A Washington *Post* story of March 7, 1968, by Bernard Nossiter, gives another very depressing report of the failure thus far of the birth control campaign in rural India. The following sample statements will give the flavor of the article:

". . . a Hindu father of three blurts out, 'It is a sin to prevent children from being born.' "

"A grizzled farmer breaks in angrily and says, 'You must practice self-control.' "

"[This] crew is responsible for fifty-nine thousand persons in more than one hundred villages. In the ten months of active campaigning only forty-seven vasectomies have been performed, twenty-seven loops inserted, and very few free condoms accepted."

What then, in summary, is the record of family planning in India? At the start of the program the Indian population growth rate was around 1.3% per year, and the population was some 370 million. After 18 years of effort at family planning, the growth rate was 2.6% per year, and the population was well over 550 million.

In fact, I know of no country in the world that has achieved true population control through family planning programs (or in any other way). The often quoted examples of Taiwan and Korea are countries undergoing demographic transition, and the role of family planning programs in reducing the birth rates is hard to estimate. But their growth rates have been slowed (2.3 and 2.5% respectively in 1970), not brought to zero.

Japan lowered its growth rate dramatically, but not through conventional family planning. A modern, industrialized nation with a highly efficient agriculture, Japan was faced after World War II with a series of cramped islands and with no opportunity to expand.

Both government and industry in Japan supported the program of population control. Its dramatic halving of the birth rate was achieved originally through the sanctioning of abortion. Abortion is a highly effective weapon in the armory of population control. It is condemned by many family planning groups, which are notorious for pussyfooting about methodology, despite their beginning 60 years ago as revolutionary social pioneers. The United Nations, for instance, does not include abortion in family planning. Quite the contrary, the U.N. justifies family planning as a method of combating abortion! Japan's industry, feeling the competition from other Asian countries with cheap labor pools, has now withdrawn its support from the population control picture. The Japanese government has issued a statement supporting the position of industry and calling for a higher birth rate. Japan is overcrowded, seriously polluted, and depends heavily on imports and fishing in order to feed its population. One can only hope that young Japanese couples have more sense than their government does.

At any rate, the situations in Taiwan, Korea, and Japan are in no way equivalent to those in most UDCs. We would be foolish in the extreme to count on similar sequences of events taking place in other parts of Asia, in Africa, or in Latin America.

Fortunately there are some signs that more UDCs and international organizations have begun to recognize the seriousness of the population situation. The U.N. has greatly increased its family planning activities, operating through several agencies including WHO, UNICEF, and UNESCO. Secretary General U Thant has been urged by a study group to establish a special "world population institute" promptly to take practical action against population growth. Robert McNamara, president of the World Bank, has put population projects high on the Bank's list of priorities. The Organization for Economic Cooperation and Development (OECD) is also getting into the field. All this is only a beginning, and so far the action has been limited to family planning. But it is a beginning and may lead to more effective action—if it isn't done too late.

What is the government of the United States doing in the area of population control? It has been bailing the sinking ship with a very small and leaky thimble. Despite repeated statements of concern since 1965 by Presidents Johnson and Nixon and various other public figures, remarkably little concrete has been done. As late as 1968, government appropriations for family planning, the bulk of which was used for research, approximately equaled appropriations for rat control. In late 1970, Congress finally passed the Family Planning Services and Population Research Act to provide free contraception to the poor through nonprofit agencies. It also established an Office of Population Affairs in the Department of Health, Education, and Welfare to sponsor further research on birth control. This is a somewhat hopeful sign in that significant amounts of money ($382 million for three years) are at last being put into birth control. However the measure is long overdue and certainly cannot by any means be called population control; it is only provision of family planning for the poor—something the affluent have had available for more than half a century. This program has not yet been funded; hopefully Congress will appropriate funds early in 1971.

Two bills oriented to population control have been introduced into both houses of Congress by Senator Robert Packwood and Congressman Paul McCloskey. One of them is a revision of income-tax laws to allow deductions for no more than two children per family. The other would completely legalize abortion. Neither of these bills seems likely to be passed in the near future, but Congress has at last been awakened to the population explosion and has begun to talk about it.

In March 1970, a two-year Commission on Population Growth and the American Future was established under the chairmanship of John D. Rockefeller, III. This commission is taking a hard look at the U.S. population, resource, and environment situation. It has already gone beyond its mandate by regarding population growth as subject to influence, not as an unalterable "given." Hopefully the Commission will come up with some strong recommendations which will be given serious consideration.

On the world front, funds for AID's family planning assistance programs have been increased from $9 million in 1967 to $100 million in 1971—certainly a move in the right direction. Increased U.S. funds have also been given to programs sponsored by international agencies such as the U.N. and the World Bank. Aside from government contributions, private foundations such as Ford and Rockefeller are becoming more involved in programs, both for research and overseas family planning projects.

But it's still less than a drop in the bucket compared to the magnitude of the problem and its significance to most of our other problems. Next to nothing is being done toward real population control in the U.S. or on a world scale. Most of the effort goes into family planning or contraceptive research—necessary but not enough.

Beginning with Senators Ernest Gruening and Joseph Clark in the middle 1960s, there has been a small group of dedicated people in Congress who have been trying to get the government to move on these matters. More recently, the ball has been carried by Senators Joseph Tydings and Robert Packwood, and Representatives Paul McCloskey, George Bush, and James Scheuer.

A few other senators and congressmen have indicated concern for population problems. If we manage to get through the coming crisis, the American people—indeed, the people of the world—will owe a great debt to these men. Their fight is uphill every inch of the way, and progress with the entrenched bureaucrats has been slow indeed. Unfortunately, many of our other legislators are still much more concerned with death control than population control.

Recently there has been a considerable flap over the legal problems involved in transplantation of human organs. Yet this problem is completely insignificant compared with those we have been considering. Unless action is taken on the population front soon, human organ transplants will become an historical curiosity— if history continues. The American people and their elected representatives must be convinced that continued preoccupation with the problems and diseases of middle age may well prevent today's youngsters from reaching that age. There has been little effective criticism of the medical profession or the government for their preoccupation with death control. That reduction of the death rate in a population will lead to disaster if the birth rate remains uncontrolled is not recognized. (One of the most important roles of sex education must be to impress on everyone that death control in the absence of birth control is self-defeating, to say the least.)

One might think that American scientists, especially biologists, would be using their influence to get the government moving. Unfortunately they are all too often a retrograde influence. The establishment in American biology and medicine consists primarily of death-controllers: those interested in intervening in population processes only by lowering death rates. They have neither the background nor the inclination to understand the problem. The prevailing attitude still seems to be that scientists should remain apolitical and that population control should not be pushed because it isn't popular with most governments. I suppose if the world's governments decree it, the laws of nature will just have to step aside and let mankind turn the universe into solid people!

Fortunately, a growing number of scientists, not only younger ones, but also some who have long been part of the establishment, have begun to make public their feelings about both the population explosion and our environmental problems. But this group has a vast load of inertia and even resistance to overcome.

General acceptance of the population situation and the need for action apparently comes hard. The idea seems finally to be filtering through to the public consciousness, at least in the U.S., thanks largely to increased coverage in the media. One seldom encounters an American who has never heard of the "population explosion" any longer. However, knowing it exists and regarding it as serious are two different things. In surveys asking people to rate the seriousness of a series of problems including the war, crime, inflation, etc., the population problem usually appears near the bottom of the list. By contrast, pollution now often appears among the top three. This lack of understanding of the connection between the two problems is confirmed by recent surveys which indicate that young women still wish and plan to have an average of more than three children.

But a new organization exists—Zero Population Growth—whose mission is to educate the public and politicians to the necessity for stopping population growth as soon as possible, to lobby for legislation, and to work for politicians who support the same goals. ZPG now has more than 30,000 members and is growing fast. Hopefully it will have developed some real political clout by 1972. Furthermore, some of the more traditional family planning organizations, particularly Planned Parenthood and the Association for Voluntary Sterilization, are now pushing the "two-child" family ideal, and taking somewhat stronger stands than before.

One of the more encouraging signs of progress has been the change in abortion laws. Since 1967, nearly one-third of the states have liberalized their abortion laws to some degree. There are four—New York, Alaska, Hawaii, and Washington state—which have "repeal" laws which allow abortion to be a matter between the woman concerned and her physician. Washington's reform was accomplished by referendum—a landmark indeed. Regularly taken polls have indicated a remarkable change in public opinion. In less than five years, disapproval of free access to abortion has become definitely a minority view.

It would be all too easy to look at these first halting steps and think the problem is solved. Lest you should be tempted, let me remind you that the U.S. birth rate is rising again, and that a minimum of 50 years will be required to halt growth even after the two-child family is established. If present growth rates continue, U.S. population will be between 270 and 285 million by the year 2000. If fertility were reduced to the replacement level by 1975, the population would stabilize at around 293 million some time between 2040 and 2050, according to estimates made by economist Stephen Enke.[36]

On the international scene, the population control situation is dismal. The principal dim sources of "hope" are the attitudes and actions of governments like those of India, Pakistan, Chile, and other UDCs, and the beginnings of consciousness shown by international agencies and a few ODCs. These few at least realize there is a problem and are trying to take action. Sweden's activity in pioneering birth control assistance to UDCs has been well ahead of other ODCs. Our own disgraceful puttering in the past really cannot be dignified even by the term "efforts." It is ironic that some Latin American politicians have accused the United States of attempting to pressure them into population control programs. If only it were true!

Multiplying Bread

In a famous 1965 speech before the United Nations, Pope Paul VI stated, "You must strive to multiply bread so that it suffices for the tables of mankind, and not, rather, favor an artificial control of birth, which would be irrational, in order to diminish the number of guests at the banquet of life." We have already seen that the "banquet of life" is, for at least one half of humanity, a breadline or worse. Let's take a look at what is being done at the moment to "multiply bread."

Is there a hope of making today's miserable existence for that half of humanity into a true banquet? Many people seem to feel that the bread can be multiplied indefinitely. A 1970 article in *Time*[37] on the Green Revolution quoted the FAO (U.N. Food and Agriculture Organization) to the effect that "the world's agricultural potential is great enough to feed 157 billion people." This is an absurd extreme of technological optimism, but it is representative of the attitudes of a large number of uninformed Americans, "experts" and nonexperts alike. I have dealt with it in detail elsewhere.[38] However, a subsequent letter to the editor of *Time* brought forth the information that the estimate originated not with the FAO but with Colin Clark, an elderly Catholic economist. Clark apparently makes his estimates by multiplying the total acreage of dry land in the world by the productivity of experimental fields in Iowa.

What are the prospects for increasing food production? Can we expect great increases to occur through the placing of more land under cultivation? The answer is a most definite *no*. In almost all instances land that is not farmed today is not farmed for excellent reasons—bad soil, lack of water, unsuitable climate, or some combination of these. In many cases attempts have been made to farm the land and they have failed.

When I talk about the population crisis to groups of businessmen, one theme reappears consistently during the question period. It is usually phrased something like this: "I just took a jet to Chicago and noticed that there is a lot of empty country in Nevada. Can't we just farm that country and greatly increase our food production?" The answer is yes and no. Yes, we could farm some of that country—we could farm the surface of the moon if we put enough money, energy, and effort into it. No, we won't do it, at least not in time to affect the coming crisis. The expense would make it economically impossible. I usually point out that supplying water to Nevada's deserts would be one of the most serious problems, though not the only one. Inevitably someone in the audience disagrees—after all, commercial desalting of the oceans is becoming a reality.

So it is. But commercial desalting, at least in the next few decades, is going to be one of those "thimble-bailing" operations. If the rosiest predictions of the commercial interests working on desalting come true, we will have a worldwide desalting capacity of 20 billion gallons a day in 1984. Pretty impressive, until you learn that the United States alone needs some 700 billion gallons of water a day in 1984—three-fourths more than the 400 billion gallons used today. That is, the maximum *world* desalting capacity will be able to supply 1/35th of the needs of *our country* in 1984. And, of course, there is always that little problem of getting the water from the seaside desalting plant 300 to 500 miles inland and almost a mile uphill. Farmers of the Nevada desert had better be prepared to pay a pretty price for the precious fluid, especially since they will be competing with home users and industry. The competition will be rugged, for if our current rape of the watersheds, our population growth, and our water use trends continue, in 1984 the United States will quite literally be dying of thirst.

Unfortunately all flat land isn't farmable. The Russians have given us a graphic example of the stupidity of attempting to put marginal land into production. In 1954 large sections of the dry plains of Kazakhstan were put into grain production. Khrushchev had hopes for this highly touted "virgin" lands program, but unfortunately the virgin was a harlot in disguise. Bad climate and other factors turned the program into a major disaster.

It is in the tropics, however, that being seduced by virgin lands is most dangerous. How often must we listen to the ignorant telling us that the population of Brazil can be fed simply by clearing and farming the Amazon Basin? Even disregarding the possible effects of such a project on our future supply of oxygen, the results of trying to farm the basin would be an unmitigated disaster. *Soils in most of the tropical areas of the world are extremely poor.* The lush forests that fill the Amazon Basin are covering a soil which, if exposed to the sun and air, will quickly become infertile or, as a result of complex chemical changes, even turn to a rocklike substance known as laterite. This has already happened over wide areas of the tropics. Those of us who have been fortunate enough to visit Angkor Wat in Cambodia have seen magnificent cities and temples built by the Khmer civilizations some 800 years ago. The construction materials were sandstone and *laterite*. Unfortunately for the Khmers, as they farmed the local land, it turned to laterite, great for building durable temples, impossible for growing food. The material that gave their civilization its enduring monument also was probably the major cause of its death!

Farming small clearings for a year or two and then letting the jungle reclaim them is the ancient method of agriculture in many areas with soils subject to laterization. At the moment it still seems to be the best way, at least until we develop an agricultural technology for dealing with lateritic soils. Laterization is continuing throughout the tropics and will doubtless proceed more rapidly as mankind gets increasingly desperate for food. Dr. Mary McNeil[39] states, "The ambitious plans to increase food production in the tropics to meet the pressure of the rapid rise of population have given too little consideration to the laterization problem and the measures that will have to be undertaken to overcome it." She goes on to describe the debacle at Iata in the Amazon Basin, where the government of Brazil attempted to found a farming community. Laterization destroyed the project as "in less than five years the cleared fields became virtually pavements of rock."

Let's turn to another panacea often mentioned. What about those "unmeasurable riches" in the sea? Unhappily, they have been measured and found wanting. The notion that we can extract vastly greater amounts of food from the sea in the near future is quite simply just another myth promoted by the ignorant or the irresponsible. Wherever I go, people ask me about our "farming" of the sea and are invariably shocked by my answer. We are not "farming" the sea today, although some preliminary research is now underway. It will be years before we will be capable of "farming" the sea on any significant scale, assuming pollution doesn't prevent it altogether. In general, man hunts the sea, and occasionally he herds its animals. About the only commercial planting and harvesting of marine crops that man does is some seaweed culture in Japan, and this is really best viewed as an extension of agriculture techniques into the sea. "Farming" the open sea will present an entirely different array of problems.

If we are ever greatly to increase our food yield from the sea, we must learn how to breed and harvest the minute plants (phytoplankton) that are the saltwater equivalents of the plants that our ancestors developed by breeding programs: wheat, corn, rice, and so forth. Then we must find a way to convert the harvest into something people will eat. Getting a high yield from the ocean means going to the primary production—to the plants—just as on land. Thus the only hope for increasing our yield from the sea many-fold lies in farming and eating its plants—something we are not doing and do not yet know how to do.

It is true that we might increase our hunting-herding yield from the sea; indeed, if we were very clever and lucky, we might manage a sustained yield of something like double that of today—perhaps even more.[40] To do so would involve research and a great deal of international cooperation to avoid polluting the sea and decreasing our take from overfishing. It would also take some changes in dietary habits, since part of the increase would have to be produced in the form of fish protein concentrate and similar somewhat-less-than-succulent delicacies. Can we expect international cooperation to increase rapidly enough to make a real dent in the problem over the next critical decade or two? I doubt it.

I suspect that international attempts to deal cooperatively with dwindling food resources will at best lead to situations such as those existing today in certain fisheries and in the international whaling industry. For years there has been an International Whaling Commission attempting to prevent the overfishing of whales. Their attempts have been a total failure. The industry has not regulated the size and composition of its catch, and as a result the most economically important whale species have been virtually exterminated. Before 1940 there were an estimated 140,000 blue whales in the oceans around Antarctica. In 1954 the total population of these whales was between 10,000 and 14,000. In 1963 the total number was down to somewhere between 650 and 2,000. Capture of blue whales has now been outlawed by the Commission, but their population size may already have been pushed below the point where it could recover even if left alone by man (and there is no reason to believe that it will be left alone). The entire history of the whaling industry has been one of moving year after year into the harvesting of smaller and smaller species.

I suspect that as the world food shortage becomes more extreme, increasing invasions of territorial waters by occasional foreign trawlers and similar incidents will develop into a massive, no-holds-barred race to harvest the sea. Careful cropping—that is, the harvesting of only the surplus fishes so that the fisheries are not exhausted—seems even less likely to occur than it did in the whaling industry. With technological concentration on attaining a maximum harvest, it would not surprise me if the sea were virtually emptied of its harvestable fishes and shellfish in a few decades or less.

We may already have passed the peak of returns with the present every-man-for-himself system. In 1969, for the first time since 1950, there was a decline in world fisheries productivity of 3%. This occurred despite intensified efforts and increasingly sophisticated fishing techniques. The per capita decline was of course higher, since the population grew 2% during that year. Whether or not the farming of tiny marine plants can contribute significantly to our food supply after the fisheries are destroyed remains to be seen. A lot will depend on how thoroughly we have poisoned the seas in the meantime.

What about some of the other panaceas, often highly touted in the public press? Certain food novelties have considerable potential—in the long run. For instance, protein-rich food can be produced by culturing microbes on petroleum, and it is theoretically possible that much of the world's protein deficit over the next several decades could be made up from this source. But the project is still in its pilot stage. Large-scale acceptance trials have not been conducted. The economics of production and distribution have not been worked out. We do not know, for instance, how the product could be provided to people in the nonpetroleum producing areas of the world, unless they had money to buy it. We won't see substantial food from petroleum in time to have much effect in the next decade or so, and, since the petroleum supply is finite, it can be no long-range cure. But with extraordinary effort it might help to provide an interim solution.

Other ways of reducing the protein deficit are being actively promoted. Work is going ahead on the production of grains with higher quality proteins—those which contain a better balance of the protein building-blocks (amino acids) that are necessary for human nutrition. This is being done both by breeding new varieties and by fortifying grain grown from traditional varieties. New protein foods are being produced by adding oilseed protein concentrates to foods based on cereals. The best known of these is Incaparina, developed by INCAP (Institute of Nutrition for Central America and Panama). It is a mixture of corn and cottonseed meal enriched with vitamins A and B. Another is CSM formula (corn, soya, milk). It is a mixture of 70% processed corn, 25% soy protein concentrate, and 5% milk solids. A third is Vita-Soy, a high-protein beverage now being marketed in Hong Kong. All of these and related products should be viewed as future "hopes," not current cures. The economics of their production and distribution are not well worked out. And, more important, the question of their general acceptability remains open. Incaparina has been available in Central America for more than a decade, but its impact, to quote the Paddock brothers, "remains insignificant." It remains insignificant in the face of determined efforts by private and commercial organizations to push its acceptance, and in spite of tremendous worldwide publicity. The Paddocks consider the principal problem to be its bland taste and texture. As they say, "The food tastes of a people are truly puzzling and as difficult to alter as their views on family planning."

Other unorthodox ways of providing more food are being discussed and tried in a few places. These range from herding animals not presently being herded, such as the South American capybara (a rodent) and the African eland (an antelope), to the culturing of algae in the fecal slime of our sewerage treatment plants. Presumably those who made the latter proposal expect someone else to eat the product. To my knowledge, most of these are not being attempted at the moment, nor is development being seriously planned.

In my opinion, the current program with the highest potential for reducing the scale of the coming famines involves the development and distribution of new high-yield varieties of food grains—the Green Revolution. Increasing the yield on land already under cultivation in this way is sociologically the easiest and ecologically the most intelligent method of "multiplying bread," although it is certainly not without its pitfalls. New rice varieties, developed primarily at the International Rice Institute, may help lift rice production in the UDCs from the present 1,000 to 1,500 pounds per acre of rough rice toward the 4,000 to 6,000 pounds produced in the United States, Japan, Italy, and other ODCs. Similar results may be expected with improved varieties of wheat and corn, many developed at the International

Maize and Wheat Improvement Center in Mexico. All of these new grains have the potential for at least doubling yields *under proper growing conditions.*

There lies the rub—proper growing conditions. The new grains produce their high yields only when they are given generous amounts of fertilizers. In ODCs the heavy use of synthetic fertilizers in recent years has led to serious pollution problems and may in the long run damage the soil more than it enriches it. The new high-yield grains also require more water, especially where several crops a year are harvested. This means large irrigation projects must be developed. Thus, putting the Green Revolution into action involves the same practices that have resulted in so much environmental disruption in the ODCs.

Besides environmental and developmental problems, the implementation of the Green Revolution involves numerous social and economic dislocations. Lester R. Brown, former Administrator of the International Agricultural Development Service, issued an early warning in 1968 of some of these problems.[41] ·

"As improved seed becomes available, the new varieties are often quickly adopted by a relatively small group of farmers—the larger, more commercial farmers who have adequate irrigation and credit. But the irrigated land suitable to new varieties is limited. And in West Pakistan, for example, lack of farm credit is limiting the distribution of available fertilizer . . .

"The rate of adoption may also be influenced by other factors. Extremely high prices for rice during the past year have stimulated interest in planting improved varieties. As output increases, prices may drop somewhat from present levels—reducing incentives to plant or carry out essential cultural practices. The increased output can also lead to problems with inadequate marketing facilities.

"Much land is not suited to the new varieties now

being disseminated. Some farmers, after trying them, will return to traditional varieties."

Many of these predicted difficulties have already materialized. Brown is extremely enthusiastic about the new varieties themselves, but he is also aware of the environmental dangers inherent in the Green Revolution. At best, he feels it can keep food production rising for perhaps another 10 to 20 years. Norman Borlaug, who won the Nobel Peace Prize for developing high-yield wheat strains, has voiced a similar opinion. Both men have repeatedly warned that the only genuine solution to the food problem is population control.

It will be a few years before really substantial estimates of the long-term value of the new grain varieties that have been rushed into production can be made. We do not know how they will do under field conditions over the long run—how resistant they will be to the attacks of pests. William Paddock[42] has presented a plant pathologist's view of the crash programs to shift to new varieties. He describes India's dramatic program of planting improved Mexican wheat. Then he continues: "Such a rapid switch to a new variety is clearly understandable in a country that totters on the brink of famine. Yet with such limited testing, one wonders what unknown pathogens await a climatic change which will give the environmental conditions needed for their growth."

Again, the ecological problem: new varieties planted in denser populations, perhaps planted several times a year; simplified communities especially ripe for disaster; and, on top of this, ominously high "inputs" of pesticides and fertilizers. We obviously are going to go ahead and take the great risks associated with the increased "inputs." We can only hope that they will be applied with great care and consciousness of the risks. Meanwhile, we would be wise to accept the more pessimistic estimates of UDC food production. We already know that it is impossible to increase food production enough to cope with continued population growth. No improvement of UDC food production can do more than delay the day of reckoning unless population control is successful. Since success with both increasing productivity and controlling population is highly problematical, it would be foolish in the extreme to plan as if both would occur. As Housman said, "Train for ill and not for good."

Protecting Our Environment

Slowly but surely the more obvious aspects of environmental deterioration are beginning to register on Americans. After all, it is pretty hard to ignore the stench that exudes from most of our open bodies of water, or the tears streaming down our cheeks as we inhale the mixture of poisonous gases and solid particles that passes for air in many of our cities. Our newspapers, magazines, and scientific journals are replete with stories on pollution and with plans to clean it up. There have been hundreds of radio and TV documentary and news features devoted to environmental problems. There have been countless speechs and demonstrations involving thousands of concerned citizens, culminating in Earth Day, April 22, 1970. It is becoming apparent that even industry has become at least conscious of pollution. The American public recently has been subjected to a plethora of advertisements on the subject of how X Company is fighting pollution. Known as "ecopornography" among environmental activists, some of this material may contain some truth, but much is deceptive, and most of it is annoying. It would be preferable if the companies spent the advertising money on real pollution control. If the effort is genuinely effective, it will be recognized. And the recognition would certainly be more seemly (and credible) coming from someone else.

Clearly, one can no longer say that public attention has not been focused on the problems of pollution. Of course, focusing on the problems and solving them are two different things. Los Angeles, for instance, has had stringent smog control laws for about 20 years. Breathed any of their air lately? In Los Angeles and similar cities human population has exceeded the carrying capacity of the environment—at least with respect to the ability of the atmosphere to remove waste. Unfortunately, Los Angeles smog laws have just barely been able to keep pace with their increasing population of automobiles (the main source of L. A. smog). It seems unlikely that much improvement can be expected in this aspect of air pollution until a major shift in our economy takes place. As long as we have an automobile industry centered on the internal combustion engine and a social system which values large, overpowered cars as status symbols, we are likely to be in trouble. It remains to be seen whether an economical, desirable car can be produced that will eliminate all the serious contaminants, including the dangerous nitrogen oxides.

Gasoline manufacturers have taken one step in the right direction by introducing unleaded gas. But that won't help unless the overwhelming majority of drivers use it. So far it costs a few cents more per gallon than leaded gas. A higher tax on leaded gas might help put unleaded gas into everyone's car. President Nixon has proposed a tax on lead additives for this purpose, but Congress has not seen fit to act on it. The city of Buffalo has banned the sale of gasoline containing more than ½ gram of lead per gallon after 1976. Some other cities, including New York, are considering similar ordinances.

On New Year's Eve 1970, President Nixon signed into law a strong clean-air bill, which had been initiated in the Senate by Senator Edmund Muskie. The act sets a deadline for the reduction by 90% of auto emissions of hydrocarbons and carbon monoxide by January 1,

1975; and of nitrogen oxides by 1976, with the possibility of one-year extensions, if necessary. It also provides for establishing and enforcing national air quality standards by 1976. The Environmental Protection Agency is empowered to take action against uncooperative industrial and government polluters, and provision is also made for citizen suits. While $1.1 billion for the first three years has been authorized for this legislation, it has not at this writing been appropriated.

President Nixon has promised vigorous enforcement of this new law; if he keeps his promise the steady decline we've had in air quality may finally be halted, possibly even somewhat reversed. But we're not out of the woods yet. How stringently pollution standards are enforced will depend to a large extent on how much the public cares. Remember, the emission standards won't take effect for five years, and the changeover in automobiles will take another five to ten years while older models are retired.

Unless the effort is successful in perfecting and producing ways to restrict smog output, our growing population of automobiles will keep Los Angeles and similar cities unfit for human habitation. The only long-term direction for the automobile industry is to move to smaller, long-lasting, recyclable cars; cars which (considering the finite nature of the petroleum supply) are powered by something other than gasoline. Meanwhile the U. S. must shift its emphasis to the development of mass transportation systems, which produce much less pollution per passenger mile and consume far less non-renewable resources. This development should be designed to absorb part of the production capacity of Detroit which will be freed as its current overproduction is phased out. The aerospace industry might also turn its resources and talents to this problem, rather than to SSTs and destructive weapons systems. Both the industries and the public would profit.

In spite of the serious nature of industrial and automotive air pollution, it is perhaps the most easily solved of our pollution problems. Factories and automobiles can be forced to meet standards of pollutant production, and I suspect that in most cases this can be done without serious economic loss. Indeed, there are already many stories of industries that have profited by selling the materials that they once gaily disgorged into the atmosphere. The recovery devices have been more than paid for by the sales. Even if there should be economic loss, it would be offset by other savings. According to the National Wildlife Federation, air pollution costs the public over $13 billion in damage per year to property, health, and crops. By contrast, less than a third of a billion dollars has budgeted for air pollution control in 1971 by industry and government agencies, just under one billion in 1972.

But even if we must pay more for our automobiles, get along with only one small car per family, or drive steam turbine or electric cars with miserable pickup, slow speed, and short range, these will be small prices for not rotting our lungs. The time "wasted" in driving slowly to the corner drugstore will be compensated by a smaller chance of being mangled before you get home, and by years of longevity tacked on to the end of your life. Think of the pleasure in living those extra years breathing clean air!

Pesticide pollution in food and elsewhere may be more difficult to deal with than air pollution. As I mentioned earlier, the immediate threat to your health from pesticides is not great. It is unlikely that you will drop dead of insecticide poisoning tomorrow; although deaths from organophosphates like parathion are common among farm workers. We are much less sure, however, what the long-term effects of the many pesticides with which we are being constantly assailed will be. We are reasonably convinced they exist, especially in the case of DDT. Most other pesticides haven't been around long enough or studied in enough detail for long-term effects to be detected. Tolerances for pesticides are set by the federal government, you say? Doesn't that protect us from their harmful effects? Hardly. First of all, most tolerances are set on the basis of short-term animal experiments and are set one poison at a time. Then, when it proves to be impossible to keep tolerances within limits, pressures are brought on the government, and the tolerances are conveniently raised. The original Food and Drug Administration (FDA) tolerances for DDT in milk fed to babies was zero. But when virtually all milk became DDT contaminated, the FDA was forced to set new tolerances.

The Rienows, in their superb book, *Moment in the Sun*,[43] describe the situation very well:

"What do all the thousands of 'minute, insignificant' tolerance-doses of chlorinated hydrocarbons, the antibiotics, organic phosphates, herbicides, hormones, systemic insecticides, rodenticides, fungicides, preservatives, arsenic additives, the omnipresent sodium nitrates and sodium nitrites, tranquilizer residues, coal tar colors, the emulsifiers, propionates, and possible carcinogens add up to in an average American's six-month diet, for instance?"

The answer is that in all probability they add up to plenty. But we'll never know for sure what the long-term effects are until the long term has passed. We won't even know then, unless the proper research programs are set up to study these effects of the various compounds, both alone and in various combinations. Studying them in combination is most important, since two compounds may act together (synergistically) in most unpleasant ways. For instance, there is growing evidence that inhaling asbestos fibers (a rather common air pollutant) and smoking cigarettes produce a greater possibility of developing lung cancer than the sum of the chances produced by asbestos or smoking alone. My guess is that a certain portion of our high mortality rates from degenerative diseases can probably be assigned to the constant assault on our cells by small doses of biologically active chemicals. I would also not be suprised if some of the mysterious "viruses" individuals complain of were actually low-level poisonings. Remember the Romans!

Americans deserve at least to know what decisions are being made for them. Perhaps the benefits of many or most of these compounds are worth whatever the increased risks are, *but those risks must be made clear.* Unfortunately, governmental programs designed to evaluate the risks, establish tolerances, and enforce the rules have been inadequate beyond belief. Look at the government's role in controlling how we and our environment are being dosed with powerful pesticides.

The Department of Agriculture (USDA) has had a long history of pushing pesticides, displaying a high level of ecological incompetence in the process. An outstanding example can be found in the history of the fire ant program. I'd like to discuss this program in some detail for two reasons. First, the action occurred long enough ago so that the results are now clear. Second, I was personally involved in the controversy about the program.

The fire ant is a nasty but not-too-serious pest in the Southeastern United States. Its nests form mounds that interfere with the working of fields. Its stings may cause severe illness or death in sensitive people, but it is a considerably smaller menace in this regard than are bees and wasps. The ant is best described as a major nuisance. After limited and inadequate research on the biology of the fire ant, the USDA in 1957 came up with the astonishing idea of carrying out a massive aerial spray campaign against the ant. Along with other biologists, including those most familiar with the fire ant,

I protested the planned program, pointing out, among other things, that the fire ant would be one of the *last* things seriously affected by a broadcast spray program. A quote from a letter I wrote concerning the problem to Ezra Taft Benson, then Secretary of Agriculture, follows:

"To any trained biologist a scorched-earth policy involving the treatment of twenty million acres with a highly potent poison such as dieldrin should be considered as a last-ditch stand, one resorted to only after all of the possible alternatives have been investigated. In addition, such a dangerous program should not even be considered unless the pest involved is an extremely serious threat to *life* and property.

"Is the Department of Agriculture aware that there are other consequences of such a program aside from the immediate death of vast numbers of animals? Is it aware that even poisoning the soil in a carefully planned strip system is bound to upset the ecological balance in the area? We are all too ignorant of the possible sequelae of such a program. Has it been pointed out that an adaptable and widespread organism such as the fire ant is one of the least likely of the insects in the treated area to be exterminated? It is also highly likely that considering its large population size, the fire ant will have the reserve of genetic variability to permit the survival of resistant strains.

"I would strongly recommend that the program be suspended: (1) until the biology of the ant can be thoroughly investigated with a view toward biological control, baiting, or some other control method superior to broadcast poisoning. and (2) until trained ecologists can do the field studies necessary to give a reasonable evaluation of the chances of success, and the concomitant damage to the human population, wildlife, and the biotic community in general of *any* contemplated control program."

I received a reply from C. F. Curl, then Acting Director of the USDA Plant Pest Control Division. Note the emphasis on "eradication" in this excerpt:

"Surveys do indicate that the imported fire ant infests approximately 20,000,000 acres in our Southern states. This does not mean, however, that the eradication program is embarked on a 'scorched-earth policy.' The infestation is not continuous, and the insecticide is applied only to areas where it is known to exist. The small outlying areas are being treated first to prevent further spread, and of the larger generally infested areas only a portion is treated in any one year.

"The method of eradication—namely, the application in granular form of two pounds of either dieldrin or heptachlor per acre—is based on an analysis of research information compiled from state and federal sources. Use experience on other control programs such as the white-fringed beetle and Japanese beetle was also taken into consideration before the final decisions were made. All the data indicated that a program could be developed which would be safe and would present a minimum of hazard to the ecological balance in the areas to be treated.

"To date, approximately 130,000 acres have been treated. This includes a block of 12,000 acres at El Dorado, Arkansas, treated nearly a year ago. Reports indicate the program is successful in eradicating the ants. No active mounds have been found in the El Dorado area, and the results look equally good in other locations treated to date. Observers vitally interested in the impact of this program to other forms of life have not reported serious disturbances to the area as a whole.

"Close liaison has been established with the Fish and Wildlife Service to continue their observations and to keep us informed currently as to the effect this program may have on fish and wildlife in the area. Experience to date indicates that a successful program can be carried out with a minimum hazard to the beneficial forms of life present.

"We believe that the points mentioned in your letter were given ample consideration before the initiation of the fire ant eradication program. We recognize, of course, that in any program where insecticides are used, certain precautions are necessary. Our experience has shown that insecticides can be applied successfully using very definite guidelines which can be established to minimize the hazard to fish and wildlife and to preclude any hazard to domestic animals and human health. Such guidelines are being followed in the operation of all control and eradication programs in which the U.S. Department of Agriculture participates."

In order to permit you to judge for yourself which one of us was right, let me quote to you parts of an article on the results of the program by Dr. William L. Brown, Jr., of the Department of Entomology of Cornell University. Dr. Brown, an outstanding biologist and a world authority on ants, wrote:[44]

"With astonishing swiftness, and over the mounting protests of conservation and other groups alarmed at the prospect of another airborne 'spray' program, the first insecticides were laid down in November, 1957. The rate of application was two pounds of dieldrin or heptachlor per acre. . . . Dieldrin and heptachlor are extremely toxic substances—about 4 to 15 times as toxic to wildlife as is DDT. Many wildlife experts and conservationists, as well as entomologists both basic and economic, felt a sense of foreboding at the start of a program that would deposit poisons with 8 to 30 times the killing power of the common forest dosage of DDT (one pound per acre in gypsy moth control).

". . . The misgivings of the wildlife people seem to have been justified on the whole, since the kill of wildlife in sample treated areas appears to have been high in most of those that have been adequately checked.

The USDA disputes many of the claims of damage, but their own statements often tend to be vague and general.

". . . Although the USDA claims that the evidence is inconclusive in some cases, there does exist contrary information indicating that stock losses from fire ant poisons may sometimes be significant.

". . . A serious blow was dealt the program in late 1958, when treatments were only one year old; Senator Sparkman and Congressman Boykin of Alabama asked that the fire ant campaign be suspended until the benefits and dangers could be evaluated properly. Then, in the beginning of 1960, the Food and Drug Administration of the Department of Health, Education, and Welfare lowered the tolerance for heptachlor residues on harvested crops to zero, following the discovery that heptachlor was transformed by weathering into a persistent and highly toxic derivative, heptachlor epoxide, residues of which turn up in meat and milk when fed to stock. Some state entomologists now definitely advise farmers against the use of heptachlor on pasture or forage.

". . . The original plan set forth in 1957 called for eradication of the ant on the North American continent, by rolling back the infestation from its borders, applying eradication measures to more central foci in the main infestation, and instituting an effective program of treatment of especially dangerous sources of spread, such as nurseries. Nearly four years and perhaps fifteen million dollars after that plan was announced, the fire ant is still turning up in new counties, and is being rediscovered in counties thought to have been freed of the pest in Arkansas, Louisiana, Florida, and North Carolina."

This rather lengthy discussion should give you some insight into two of the government agencies that should be most active in preserving the quality of our environment. The USDA, against the advice of the most competent people in the field, launched a fruitless eradication campaign which could have positive results only for the stockholders of pesticide companies. The FDA discovered another of its tolerance levels was established at the wrong level. How many of today's tolerance levels do you suppose are mis-set?

Lest you be left with the impression that the USDA is manned only by ecological incompetents, let me in fairness point out that some of the most ecologically sophisticated pest control programs have been initiated by the Department. Perhaps the most brilliant was that against the screwworm, a fly which can be an extremely serious pest on cattle. Annual losses in livestock have been estimated to be as high as $40 million a year. Under the leadership of Dr. E. F. Knipling, the USDA embarked on a massive program of sterilizing male screwworm flies and releasing them in infested areas. The female screwworm mates only once. By flooding infested areas with sterile males, the screwworm was effectively eradicated from the United States. The effectiveness of this "biological control" program makes an interesting contrast with the futile and destructive fire ant fiasco.

At the moment I am afraid that, rather than protecting our environment from deterioration, the USDA still, in the balance, is furthering that deterioration. It is still much too ready to yield to the pressures to take the chemical quick way out, to keep food esthetically appealing instead of poison-free. The setting of tolerances by the FDA is much too open to error (as can be seen by repeated readjustments), and the power available to enforce tolerances is completely inadequate. Less than one-third of 1% of the produce that you eat has been subject to federal inspection for pesticide residues, and even that small portion may well have been coated, post-inspection, by overzealous storekeepers trying to discourage flies in their supermarkets. I well remember being warned years ago by an economic entomologist employed by the state of Kansas not to eat asparagus one year. It turned out that the farmers were spraying far beyond the official tolerances, knowing that the chances of being caught were practically nil. Such occurrences are not rare and will not become rare until adequate inspection systems are established.

In 1970, the USDA announced a new program against the fire ant, involving a new, powerful insecticide, Mirex, which was to be discharged from airplanes over no less than 150 million acres in nine states during a 12-year period. Obviously some people never learn! This time, however, the USDA met with more than isolated objections from the halls of ivy.

In the late 1960s a new organization, the Environmental Defense Fund (EDF), was formed. Originally it consisted exclusively of lawyers and biologists, although its membership is now much broader, and its specific purpose (to quote one of its founders, attorney Victor Yannacone) was to "sue the bastards!" And that is precisely what it has been doing. When the new fire ant program was announced, EDF, together with several conservation groups, filed suit with the Justice Department. At this writing, the Justice Department has attacked the suit on legalistic grounds. However, the USDA spray program has been halted until the case has been tried.

EDF deserves much of the credit for what little control has been established recently over the use of DDT and other pesticides. As a result of hearings held at EDF's instigation, DDT has been banned in the states of Wisconsin and Michigan. Following those events and under resultant public pressure, the state of California and the USDA have put a series of restrictions on the use of DDT within their jurisdictions. Canada has banned DDT for 90% of usage, the USSR has stopped manufacturing it, Sweden has put a two-year moratorium on its use in that country, and 15 European countries are considering joint regulations to be established over pesticides. Interestingly, the USDA restrictions on DDT and other insecticides and herbicides, while receiving much publicity, have been much less effective and thorough than those of other countries. Where specific restrictions have been imposed, they have often been ignored or avoided through loopholes. Many restrictions applied where the named pesticide wasn't being used anyway. Most of the DDT (two-thirds) in the U.S. has been used to protect the cotton crop; until January 1971 there were no restrictions on DDT in cotton-growing areas. Then, under pressure from the U.S. Court of Appeals, after hearing a suit against DDT by EDF, the Environmental Protection Agency announced that it intended to cancel registrations of DDT and a herbicide, 2,4,5-T, if a review found both substances present "imminent hazards" to the public. The U.S. may at last ban DDT.

Since the first DDT hearings, EDF has branched out into other subjects for environmental litigation. Among them are the protection of endangered species of wildlife (including whales), suits against air polluters, action to establish noise and environmental standards for the SST, action against leaded gasolines, and action to block unnecessary development projects such as the Florida Barge Canal and the damming of the last free-running river in Arkansas. Many of these have been successful; others are still undecided.

Laws and programs designed to restore our national open sewer systems to the status of rivers and lakes have been inadequate in the extreme. In the past decade or so concern has increased, and increasing numbers of influential people have been pushing in the right direction. But until recently at least, the greed and stubbornness of industries, the recalcitrance of city governments, the weakness of state control agencies, and the general apathy of the American people have combined to keep progress discouragingly slow. One reason for the ineffectiveness of state pollution control boards may be that many representatives of potential polluters sit on them, according to a 1970 survey by the *New York Times*. Representatives of polluting industries and local governments often even participate in decisions regulating their own industries or municipalities, a rather obvious example of conflict of interest.

What the government has been up against in trying to get some industries to stop destroying our country is described in detail by reporter Frank Graham, Jr., in his fine book *Disaster by Default*.[45] Particularly instructive is the story of the great Mississippi fish kill in the early 1960s. Rough estimates give the total loss in the four years 1960–1963 as between 10 and 15 million fishes in the lower Mississippi and its bypass, the Atchafalaya.[46] The fishes killed included several kinds of catfishes, menhaden, mullet, sea trout, drum, shad, and buffalo. The die-offs were ruinous to the local fishing industry. A thorough investigation by government (Public Health Service) and private laboratories placed the blame primarily on the highly toxic insecticide endrin and one of its derivatives. It was found not only in the blood and tissues of dying fishes and water birds, but also in the mud in areas where fishes were dying. Extracts made both from the mud and from the tissues of dying fishes killed healthy fishes in experiments. Fish kills were greatest in 1960 and 1963, smallest in 1961 and 1962. Endrin was used commonly to treat cotton and cane fields in the lower Mississippi Valley in 1960 and 1963; very little was used in 1961 and 1962.

The finger of the Public Health Service pointed to waste from the Velsicol Chemical Corporation's Memphis plant as one major source of the endrin, the other being run-off from agricultural lands following dusting and spraying. Waste endrin from the manufacturing process was getting into the river. The reaction of the Velsicol Corporation should come as no surprise. Graham in *Disaster by Default*[47] described the action:

"Velsicol, under fire, shot back. Bernard Lorant, the company's vice-president in charge of research, issued strong denials. In a statement to the press, he said that endrin had nothing to do with the Mississippi fish kill, that the symptoms of the dying fish were not those of endrin poisoning, and that Velsicol's tests proved that the fish had died of dropsy."

"Dropsy"—isn't that quaint! All you tropical fish fanciers can check that one out. Turn to page 61 of your copy of William T. Innes's *Exotic Aquarium Fishes* (19th Edition), edited by Professor George S. Myers, one of the world's most renowned experts on fishes. Under "Dropsy" we read: "The puzzling thing about the malady is the unaccountable way in which it singles out individual fishes. It is *never epidemic*." (My emphasis.) Add to this the facts cited above, and the small point that the fishes had the symptoms of endrin poisoning, and we have a great natural miracle. By coincidence, perhaps ten million fishes simultaneously contracted a new form of dropsy with the symptoms of endrin poisoning. In order to fool investigators they produced endrin in their tissues and excreted it into the mud of the Mississippi. Let's just hope that the approximately one million humans who drink that heady Mississippi brew don't come down in future years with a new form of "dropsy," which is delayed in its appearance and tries to fool you by having the symptoms of cirrhosis of the liver.

At a 1964 conference on the fish kill, a common theme promoted by our giants of the pesticide industry was very much in evidence: that only Communist sympathizers criticize the way pesticides are thrown around. A reading of Graham's fine book will quickly unite you with the fishermen of Mississippi, the dwellers on the shores of "Sewer Erie," and many others in the belief that the American people have powerful enemies in addition to the Communists.

Today the polluter's arguments are more sophisticated and a little closer to reality. Defenders of pesticides point with pride to the success of insecticide programs in controlling malaria and other insect-borne diseases and in raising agricultural production. They claim that halting the use of DDT and other pesticides would result in a catastrophic rise in deaths from disease and starvation. These dire predictions rest on a kernel of truth. The benefits we have gained from pesticides are undeniable; but they have not been without cost—costs we will be paying for a long time in the future, whether or not pesticides are controlled. In making a change from present practices to a more sensible regime of pest control— relying mainly on such alternatives as biological or cultural control and the very sparing use of less dangerous chemicals—we may well have to accept temporarily reduced crop production until the natural enemies of pests can be reestablished. Alternatives for disease control are even more available; however, they are more expensive in the short run.

The story is depressingly the same with other polluters. The struggles of the government over a decade to get cooperation from cities and slaughterhouses on the Missouri River to abate the hideous pollution of the river with blood, guts, hair, and "paunch manure" (undigested stomach contents) are a typical example. In 1957 Omaha city officials said they would cooperate. In 1965 the city was still dumping 300,000 pounds of untreated paunch manure and quantities of grease into the river. Sewage pollution in Raritan Bay, New Jersey, concentrated by clams, led to an epidemic of hepatitis. The clamming industry in the bay was closed down. Tough luck for the clammers. Tough luck for those who like to eat clams. Very tough luck for those who did and contracted hepatitis. No one protects the rights of fishermen, swimmers, or just the poor benighted souls who don't like the stink and slime. But then perhaps nothing in our Constitution guarantees our senses protection from loathsome assault.

The story of industrial pollution in Lake Michigan, of sewage pollution in the Hudson, and of acid pollution in Pennsylvania streams by strip miners reads much the same. Some small progress has been made in water pollution abatement and more can be expected as federal efforts to upgrade sewage treatment increase. But overall the situation is still going downhill. So far the Nixon Administration has pushed mainly for secondary sewage treatment plants, which is a wholly inadequate solution. Water treated in this way still contains the phosphates and nitrates that have led to the ruin of Lake Erie and many other of our waterways. Such water is unsuitable for recreation, irrigation, or even industrial use. I for one certainly wouldn't want to drink it!

One important move has been in forcing detergent manufacturers to switch to biodegradable chemicals which can be more readily broken down by natural processes than were previous ingredients. Even that problem has not been solved, however. The phosphates in detergents are a major element in water pollution. So some detergent manufacturers have replaced phosphates with nitrilotriacetic acid (NTA), which may be even more dangerous. In high concentrations NTA may dissolve heavy metals, such as mercury and cadmium, and keep them circulating in water systems. In combination with other common water polluting agents, it can break down into highly carcinogenic (cancer inducing) substances. A few products have appeared on the market which are biodegradable and free of phosphates or NTA. Some local governments have banned detergents containing phosphates, usually because of acute local water

pollution problems. Nassau County in New York instituted such a ban in 1970; Chicago's and Akron's go into
effect in mid-1972. Canada has put restrictions on the
amount of phosphates permitted in laundry detergents
—a limit of 20%. Under continuing public pressure, the
large detergent manufacturers may be forced to come up
with safer formulas.

The war against another kind of pollution deserves
mention here: noise pollution. It is getting considerable
attention from the designers of dwellings, factories, and
office buildings, but not as much attention as it should
be getting. And the sources of noise—the motorcycles,
power mowers, jet transports, TV sets, trucks, and so
forth—multiply merrily on with the population. There
is considerable evidence that excessive noise levels are
harmful in a number of ways, including permanent hearing loss after long exposure.

We will cross a new threshold in deafening horror if
the Federal Aviation Administration and a small segment of the aircraft and airline industries are permitted
to proceed with their preposterous supersonic transport
(SST) project. I am a pilot. I have lots of friends who
are pilots, including airline pilots. I've yet to run into
one who thinks that the SST is sensible or necessary.

Aviation has colossal needs. It needs improved airports with adequate runways and clear approaches, lo-
cated far enough from major cities so that dangerous
noise abatement procedures can be dispensed with. At
some airports these procedures require reducing power
at a critical stage of takeoff in order to protect the ears
and sleep of people living nearby. Aviation also needs
fast, convenient ground transport to these terminals, and
improved air traffic control procedures. It needs just
about everything except airplanes which, if operated
over the continent, will subject Americans to a shocking
succession of sonic booms. It needs just about every-

thing except airplanes that will deposit their contrails so high in the atmosphere that they will lie above the layers of air which are regularly mixed, and thus will persist. The SST represents a beautiful example of the runaway stupidity that can characterize the end of a technological trend. A major criterion of a good airplane has almost always been how fast it can fly. After the SST we'll doubtless move on to orbital transports that will circle the earth before reentering, cutting the time from the Mojave Desert to Cape Kennedy to a mere hour (Los Angeles–New York will probably remain from five to six hours even then). If 175 SSTs were flying our domestic air routes, people living along those routes would be subjected to 700 sonic booms a day—a boom on the average of every two minutes or so. It is quite a measure of our civilization that in order to save a few people an hour or so in crossing the country (in less comfort than in a subsonic jet) we would subject millions to extreme disturbance and property damage—to say nothing of possibly contributing significantly to environmental catastrophe.

Resistance to the SST is gathering strength, however, particularly in the U.S. Senate, where Senator William Proxmire has led the fight against it. Several conservation groups, including the Sierra Club and Friends of the Earth, have been actively lobbying against it. The Nixon Administration has declared that SSTs will not be permitted to fly over the continental U.S. But if they don't, it seems evident that there will not be a large enough market to justify the expenditure. Whether such a market would exist even if they did fly over populated areas is far from clear. Several very distinguished economists have concluded that the SST program is without economic merit. In December 1970, the Senate voted against further funding of the project. In the House-Senate Conference meetings enough funds were restored to the project to carry it for three months longer. In March 1971 the question will have to be decided again. Maybe, with luck, we can still destroy this monster before it gets off the ground.

One of President Nixon's first statements after his inauguration as president in 1969 was that it was "now or never" for Americans to solve their environmental problems and that this was among his top priorities. Since then the public has seen an interesting series of hirings, firings, and reshuffling of agencies involved with environmental affairs. Secretary of the Interior Walter Hickel, who was given a rough initiation by the Senate, proved to be the most vigorous secretary we've ever had in taking polluting industries to task—particularly the oil industry. His proposed successor Rogers Morton, whose nomination has been greeted with somewhat less than wild enthusiasm by environmental groups, will have a lot to live up to.

Early in 1970, the Council on Environmental Quality was established in the President's Executive Office. Soon afterward, the CEQ issued a report which superficially listed our environmental problems but offered no serious programs for dealing with them other than to recommend a national land use policy. Other government agencies have been required to submit reports on the environmental impact of new projects to the CEQ for review, but the rumor is that many aren't bothering. Moreover, these reports are not to be released to the public until after the project has been approved, thus hampering public monitoring of the CEQ's performance.

In July 1970, the President proposed the creation of two new agencies which would absorb some of the activities of older ones. Pollution monitoring and control for air and water, solid waste management, regulation of pesticides and radiation have all been centralized into an independent Environmental Protection Agency. This new agency is also responsible for ecological research and the development of environmental policy. The first administrator is William D. Ruckelshaus, a politician and administrator who has no particular background in environmental affairs (but then, neither did Walter Hickel). The other new agency is the National Ocean and Atmospheric Administration, which was created within the Department of Commerce to unify research and other matters pertaining to the ocean and atmosphere.

Whether this reorganization of government regulating agencies will result in more effective federal action in dealing with the environment remains to be seen. But some important roadblocks to action have been removed simply by transferring the power to license or ban pesticides away from the Department of Agriculture and transferring the regulation of nuclear power and radioactive wastes away from the Atomic Energy Commission. Given appropriate funds and support from Congress, the President, and the public, the Environmental Protection Agency has the potential to evolve into a powerful friend of our environment.

Nevertheless, in an age when the most significant problems of humanity lie in the areas of ecology and the behavioral sciences, it is extraordinary that the President of the United States has not appointed a single behavioral scientist or biologist, let alone ecologist, as his advisor, as a member of the CEQ, or as head of either of the two new agencies. His science advisors have been a physicist and an electrical engineer. Is it any wonder that, at least from outward appearances, the President still does not appear to grasp the true magnitude of the environmental crisis?

In some ways more effective and more encouraging than government action has been the rise of citizen activity in behalf of the environment. Actually, the manifestation of public concern is undoubtedly a major factor in the increase of government action, and it unquestionably will continue to be an important influence. Among the most effective environmental action groups has been the EDF, already described. Some of the older, formerly conservative conservation groups, such as the Sierra Club and the Audubon Society, have also taken to the courts, often in conjunction with EDF. They have moreover become more actively involved in influencing legislation at the local, state, and federal levels, along with newer, more militant groups such as Environmental Action, Friends of the Earth, Environment!, and ZPG. The Nature Conservancy has been buying up land in an effort to preserve undeveloped wilderness for our children before it's too late. There has also been a proliferation of local and statewide organizations working in behalf of our ailing environment. Many of these groups are working for stiffer local pollution control laws and effective enforcement for them where they exist. Some have opposed unnecessary or potentially polluting development projects such as dams and power plants, especially nuclear plants. Some have simply tried to save small pieces of land for parks or wildlife refuges. Some of these projects have failed, but many have been successful.

Some organizations are primarily interested in publicizing our environmental problems. While Ralph Nader and his Raiders have been chiefly concerned with defending the American consumer against corporate abuse and government neglect, they have also shown how this abuse and neglect results in rampant pollution.

Some new organizations—particularly Ecology Action —and many local ones stress the personal approach. These groups organize recycling operations for everything from newspapers to glass to scrap metal, push biodegradable, phosphate-free detergents, and generally try to persuade people to adopt a more ecologically sane life-style. So far they have been successful mainly among students, but many of their ideas are beginning to appear in the newspapers and magazines of the establishment.

A few environmental activists prefer to go it alone: notably the Fox. This gentleman, who lives in a Chicago suburb, has declared a sort of underground, one-man war against industrial pollution. Among his achievements are capping a smokestack, plugging a sewer outlet, and dumping 50 pounds of raw sewage on the reception room floor of the company that had put it in the river. The Fox may not have stopped any pollution directly, but he has certainly succeeded in making people in Chicago aware of it and embarrassing a number of polluters.

The new environmental movement has been successful in generating something else: opposition from an unexpected quarter—the minorities. In emphasizing such threatened middle-class values as the right to hunt and fish and retreat to the wilderness, the movement has neglected to include the very real environmental degradation of slums and ghettos. Perhaps we should not be surprised then that black militants and other minority leaders have not enthusiastically hopped onto the environmental bandwagon, but on the contrary often regard the movement as yet another diversion of money and action from programs to meet their needs.

Ironically, it is these same people who suffer most from some kinds of environmental deterioration and stand to gain the most from any improvements. Apart from the physical, unsanitary wretchedness of slum living, ghettos in the city centers are often in the areas of heaviest air pollution. Negroes in the U.S. have higher DDT residues in their bodies than whites on the average. The reason is unknown; possibly it has to do with poorer diets. Chicano farm workers are exposed to much higher levels of pesticides and other farm chemicals than the rest of the population. The environment movement must recognize this and include the improvement of conditions for the poor as well as the middle classes as an essential part of its campaign.

What is happening outside the United States? Compared to our feeble efforts, not much. Environmental deterioration has become a subject for discussion in the U.N., but little more. The World Health Organization, on the other hand, refuses to give up DDT for malaria control, claiming that hundreds of millions are doomed without it. Officials of many developing countries point with pride to the smog over their cities as a sign of progress.

Japan, whose air pollution has reached the point where oxygen dispensing machines are available on city street corners, and policemen are required to use them on bad days, is just beginning to wake up. At the end of 1970, the government passed the first serious antipollution legislation, making it a criminal offense to pollute.

Some European countries have had some success in pollution control, but the situation there is also getting out of hand. There have recently been some tentative movements toward action on a regional basis, particularly for the control of pesticides. England and France are having second thoughts about their SSTs.

Canada's environmental concern has fairly nearly paralleled that of the U.S. In areas of pesticides and detergents, she is ahead of us. She is also quite justifiably alarmed about U.S. designs on her water resources and oil and mineral resources in the far north. Not surprisingly, Canada is watching the Alaskan oil development controversy with considerable interest.

What, then, is being done overall to nurse our sick environment back to health? How well are we treating these symptoms of the Earth's disease of overpopulation? Are we getting ahead of the filth, corruption, and noise? Are we guarding the natural cycles on which our lives depend? Are we protecting ourselves from subtle and chronic poisoning? The answer is obvious—the palliatives are still too few and too weak. The patient continues to get sicker.

Chapter 4
WHAT NEEDS TO BE DONE?

A general answer to the question, "What needs to be done?" can be given easily. We must rapidly bring the world population under control, reducing the growth rate to zero and eventually making it go negative. Conscious regulation of human numbers must be achieved. Simultaneously we must greatly increase our food production. This agricultural program should be carefully monitored to minimize deleterious effects on the environment and should include an effective program of ecosystem restoration. The world's supply of nonrenewable resources must be assessed and plans made for the most economical and beneficial management and use of what remains of them. As these projects are carried out, an international policy research program must be initiated to set optimum population-environment goals for the world and to devise methods for reaching these goals. So the answer to the question is simple. Getting the job done, unfortunately, is going to be complex beyond belief—if indeed it can be done. What follows in this chapter are some ideas on how these goals *might* be reached and a brief evaluation of our chances of reaching them.

Getting Our House in Order

The key to the whole business, in my opinion, is held by the United States. We are the most influential superpower; we are the richest nation in the world. At the same time we are also just one country on an ever-shrinking planet. It is obvious that we cannot exist unaffected by the fate of our fellows on the other end of the good ship Earth. If their end of the ship sinks, we shall at the very least have to put up with the spectacle of their drowning and listen to their screams. Communications satellites guarantee that we will be treated to the sights and sounds of mass starvation on the evening news, just as we have seen Vietnamese corpses being disposed of in living color and listened to the groans of American wounded. We're unlikely, however, to get off with just our appetites spoiled and our consciences disturbed. If we have any surplus food to give away at all, the amounts will not be large—and if we are unlucky we may be short ourselves. Our GNP will have grown relative to that of the UDCs, although the quality of our lives will have diminished. But the hungry nations will not care that our situation is worsening. They will focus on the ever-larger economic gap.

Can we guess what effect this growing disparity will have on our "shipmates" in the UDCs? Will they starve gracefully, without rocking the boat? Or will they attempt to overwhelm us in order to get what they consider to be their fair share?

We, of course, cannot remain affluent and isolated. At the moment the United States uses about one-third of all the raw materials consumed each year. Think of it: less than 1/15th of the population of the world requires about five times its "fair share" to maintain its inflated position. If present trends continue, in 20 years we will be much less than 1/15th of the population, and yet we may use some 50% of the resources consumed. Our affluence depends heavily on many different kinds of imports: ferroalloys (metals used to make various kinds of steel), tin, bauxite (aluminum ore), rubber, and so forth. Will other countries, many of them in the grip of starvation and anarchy, still happily supply these materials to a nation that cannot give them food? Even the technological optimists don't think we can free ourselves of the need for imports, so we're going to be up against it.

So, beside our own serious population problem at home, we are intimately involved in the world crisis. We are involved through our import-export situation. We are involved because of the possibilities of global ecological catastrophe, of global pestilence, and of global thermonuclear war. Also, we are involved because of the humanitarian feelings of most Americans.

We are going to face some extremely difficult but unavoidable decisions. By how much, and at what environmental risk, should we increase our domestic food production in an attempt to feed the starving? How much should we reduce the grain-finishing of beef in order to have more food for export? How will we react when asked to balance the lives of a million Latin Americans against, say, a 30 cent per pound rise in the average price of beef? Will we be willing to slaughter our dogs and cats in order to divert pet food protein to the starving masses in Asia? If these choices are presented one at a time, out of context, I predict that our behavior will be "selfish." Men do not seem to be able to focus emotionally on distant or long-term events. Immediacy seems to be necessary to elicit "selfless" responses. Few Americans could sit in the same room with a child and watch it starve to death. But the death of several million children this year from starvation is a distant, impersonal, hard-to-grasp event. You will note that I put quotes around "selfish" and "selfless." The words describe the behavior only out of context. The "selfless" actions necessary to aid the rest of the world and stabilize the population are our only hope for survival. The "selfish" ones work only toward our destruction. Ways must be found to bring home to all the American people the reality of the threat to their way of life—indeed, to their very lives.

Obviously our first step must be immediately to establish and advertise drastic policies designed to bring our own population size under control. We must define a goal of a stable optimum population size for the United States and display our determination to move rapidly toward that goal. Such a move does two things at once. It improves our chances of obtaining the kind of country and society we all want, and it sets an example for the world. The second step is very important, as we also are going to have to adopt some very unpopular foreign policy positions relative to population control, and we must do it from a psychologically strong position. We will want to disarm one group of opponents at the outset: those who claim that we wish *others* to stop breeding while we go merrily ahead. We want our propaganda based on "do as we do"—not "do as we say."

So the first task is population control at home. How do we go about it? Many of my colleagues feel that some sort of compulsory birth regulation would be necessary to achieve such control. One plan often mentioned involves the addition of temporary sterilants to water supplies or staple food. Doses of the antidote would be carefully rationed by the government to produce the desired population size. Those of you who are appalled at such a suggestion can rest easy. The option isn't even open to us, since no such substance exists. If the choice now is either such additives or catastrophe, we shall have catastrophe. It might be possible to develop such population control tools, although the task would not be simple. Either the additive would have to operate equally well and with minimum side effects against both sexes, or some way would have to be found to direct it only to one sex and shield the other. Feeding potent male hormones to the whole population might sterilize and defeminize the women, while the upset in the male population and society as a whole can be well imagined. In addition, care would have to be taken to see to it that the sterilizing substance did not reach livestock, either through water or garbage.

Technical problems aside, I suspect you'll agree with me that society would probably dissolve before sterilants were added to the water supply by the government. Just consider the fluoridation controversy! Some other way will have to be found. Another possibility might be to reverse the government's present system of encouraging reproduction and replace it with a series of financial rewards and penalties designed to discourage reproduction. For instance, we could change our present system of tax exemptions, as advocated in Senator Packwood's bill. Since taxes in essence purchase services from the government, and since large families require more services, why not make them pay for them? The present system was designed at a time when larger population size was not viewed as undesirable. But no sane society should promote larger population size today. The new system would be quite simple, but, of course, not retroactive! Senator Packwood's original proposal allowed a deduction of $1,000 for the first child, $750 for the second, $500 for the third, and none for subsequent children. This would apply only to children born after January 1, 1973, with previously born children continuing to receive deductions that applied before the new law would take effect. Other adjustments have been made to avoid penalizing low-income families. Since the bill was first proposed, the deduction for the third child has been removed. In short, the plush life would be difficult to attain for those with large families—which is as it should be, since they are getting their pleasure from their children, who are being supported in part by more responsible members of society.

On top of the income tax change, luxury taxes could be placed on layettes, cribs, diapers, diaper services, expensive toys, always with the proviso that the essentials be available without penalty to the poor. There would, of course, have to be considerable experimenting on the level of financial pressure necessary to achieve the population goals. To the penalties could be added some incentives. A governmental "first marriage grant" could be awarded each couple in which the age of both partners was 25 or more. "Responsibility prizes" could be given to each couple for each five years of childless marriage, or to each man who accepted irreversible sterilization (vasectomy) before having more than two children. Or special lotteries might be held—tickets going only to the childless. Adoption could be subsidized and made a simple procedure. Considering the savings in school buildings, pollution control, unemployment compensation, and the like, these grants would be a money-making proposition. But even if they weren't, the price would be a small one to pay for saving our nation.

Obviously, such measures should be coordinated by a powerful governmental agency. A federal Bureau of Population and Environment should be set up to determine the optimum population size for the United States and devise measures to establish it. Of course this should be done within the context of resource and environmental limitations. The BPE should coordinate population policies with those dealing with environmental protection and resource husbandry. This Bureau should be given ample funds to support research in the areas of population control and environmental quality. In the first area it would promote intensive investigation and development of new techniques of birth control. This research will not only give us better methods to use at home, which will be essential for helping the UDCs to control their populations: the BPE also would encourage more research on human sex determination, for if a simple method could be found to guarantee that first-born children were males, then population control problems in many areas would be somewhat eased. In our country and elsewhere, couples with only female children "keep trying" in hope of a son.

Two other functions of the BPE would be to aid Congress in developing legislation relating to population and environment, and to inform the public of the needs for such legislation. Some of these needs are already apparent. The right of *any* woman to have an abortion if it is approved by a physician should be guaranteed. We need federal legislation affirming the right to voluntary sterilization for adults of both sexes and protecting physicians who perform such operations from legal harassment. We need a federal law requiring sex education in schools—sex education that includes discussion of the need for regulating the birth rate and of the techniques of birth control. Such education should begin at the earliest age recommended by those with professional competence in this area—certainly before junior high school.

By "sex education" I do not mean course focusing on hygiene or presenting a simple-minded "birds and bees" approach to human sexuality. The reproductive function of sex must be shown as just one of its functions, and one that must be carefully regulated in relation to the needs of the individual and society. Much emphasis must be placed on sex as an interpersonal relationship, as an important and extremely pleasurable aspect of being human, as mankind's major and most enduring recreation, as a fountainhead of humor, as a phenomenon that affects every aspect of human life. Contrary to popular mythology, sex is one of our *least* "animal" functions. First of all, many animals (and plants) get along without any sex whatever. They reproduce asexually. It is clear from biological research that sex is not primarily a mechanism of reproduction; it is a mechanism that promotes variability. In many organisms which do have sexual processes, these processes occur at a stage in the life cycle that is not the stage at which reproduction occurs. And, of course, no other animal has all of the vast cultural ramifications of sex that have developed in human society. In short, sex, as we know it, *is a peculiarly human activity.* It has many complex functions other than the production of offspring. It is now imperative that we restrict the reproductive function of sex while producing a minimum of disruption in the others.

Fortunately, there are hopeful signs that the anti-human notions that have long kept Western society in a state of sexual repression no longer hold sway over many of our citizens. With a rational atmosphere mankind should be able to work out the problems of deemphasizing the reproductive role of sex. These problems include finding substitutes for the satisfaction and rewards that women derive from childbearing and for the ego satisfaction that often accompanies excessive fatherhood. Implicit attitudes and social pressures within our society toward parenthood, especially motherhood, add up to an even more powerful pronatal policy than our legal system represents. Equal opportunities and salaries for women in business and the professions, which are now being sought by the women's liberation movement, would strongly encourage them to seek other outlets for their energy and talents besides motherhood. Society would greatly benefit both from the resulting lowered fertility and the productive contributions of the women.

All too often today marriage either provides a "license" for sexual activity or a way of legitimizing the unplanned results of premarital sexual activity. But greater equality between the sexes, reliable contraceptives, and changing attitudes among today's young people are solving the former problem; the greater availability of contraceptives and abortion could solve the latter. Marriage should be entered into as a positive relationship, perhaps including the provision of a proper environment for rearing children; not because it is "the thing to do." Countless people today marry and/or have children more as a result of social pressure from friends and their own parents than from any positive desire of their own. Simply removing those pressures might take us a long way toward lower birth rates.

If we take the proper steps in education, legislation, and research, we should be able in a generation to have a population thoroughly enjoying its sexual activity, while raising physically and mentally healthier children, but in smaller numbers. The population should be relatively free of the horrors created today by divorce, illegal abortion, venereal disease, and the psychological pressures of a sexually repressive and repressed society. Much, of course, needs to be done, but support for action in these directions is becoming more and more common in the medical profession, the clergy, and the public at large. If present trends can be continued, we should be able to minimize and in some cases reverse social pressures against population control at home and to influence those abroad in the same direction.

Of course, this enlightened atmosphere does not exist

today. Potent forces still must be overcome if we are to get the attitude of our government changed in the area of population control.

Although the performance and attitudes of American Catholics relative to the use of birth control are similar to those of non-Catholics, conservative elements in the Church hierarchy still resist change. The Papal Encyclical of 1968 reconfirmed this conservative stance. The degree to which this goes against the attitudes of American Catholics was revealed in a Gallup Poll taken in late 1965. Of the Catholics questioned, 56 percent expressed the opinion that the Church should change its opinion on methods of birth control, while only 33 percent thought it should not change. Opinion among intellectual Catholics seems even more heavily in favor of a change in the Church's position.

A Catholic colleague, Dr. John H. Thomas, has written, "My first duty as a Catholic is to do what I believe is morally correct. There is no doubt in my mind that the position of the Church with respect to birth control is morally wrong. The price of doctrinaire insistence on unworkable methods of birth control is high. It contributes to misery and starvation for billions, and perhaps the end of civilization as we know it. As a scientist I also know that Catholic doctrine in this area is without biological foundation. It is therefore my duty both to myself and to the Church not just to ignore this doctrine, but to do everything within my power to change it. After all, without drastic worldwide measures for population control in the near future, there will be no Church anyway. If the Church, or, for that matter, any organized religion, is to survive, it must become much more humanitarian in focus. If it does, the theology will take care of itself."

The announcement of the papal encyclical *Humanae Vitae* was greeted by a great wave of protest from within the Catholic Church. This dissent was not limited to lay people; it existed throughout the clergy as far up into the hierarchy as the rank of cardinal. Most of the dissent centered in Europe, especially the Netherlands, France, and Germany, and in the U.S. A cathedral in Washington, D.C., was picketed and boycotted. There was a small amount of protest in South America, but the more usual reaction was to proceed with family planning programs (some of which operate with clerical cooperation) as if nothing had happened. Ignorance and poverty are such in some areas of South America that women flocked to their priests and demanded to know, "What is this pill the Pope is against?"

A few months after the encyclical was issued, a group of scientists circulated a statement of protest at a national scientific convention. In part, the statement said:

"It is high time, therefore, that we make our stand on the birth control encyclical perfectly clear. We pledge that we will no longer be impressed by pleas for world peace or compassion for the poor from a man whose deeds help to promote war and make poverty inevitable. The world must quickly come to realize that Pope Paul VI has sanctioned the deaths of countless numbers of human beings with his misguided and immoral encyclical. The fact that this incredible document was put forth in the name of a religious figure whose teachings embodied the highest respect for the value of human dignity and life should serve to make the situation even more repugnant to mankind."

Well over a thousand scientists signed the statement at the meetings and hundreds more have signed it since. Among these were hundreds of Catholics, several Nobel Prize winners, and many scientists from outside the United States. A copy of the statement was sent to the Pope along with a list of those who signed it.

Despite widespread disagreement with the encyclical, many Catholics are still opposed to attempts to institute even the most inadequate government programs of population control. Catholic politicians at home and abroad have operated in many ways to obstruct population control. They have often effectively blocked action at the international level. And population control, of course, is the *only* solution to problems of population growth. Unless the Pope does a complete about-face, I think we can count on his continuing support for raising the death rate.

This encouragement of high death rates through political interference is now the most important role of the Church in the population crisis. There is little reason to believe that, if obstructionist behavior by the hierarchy and other influential Catholics ceased, *performance* of Catholic couples would differ significantly from that of non-Catholics in most areas. Furthermore, in the UDCs outside of Latin America, Catholics are rarely a significant portion of the problem. It is a mistake to focus too strongly on the Catholic element in the population situation. True, we must bring pressure to bear on the Pope in hope of getting a reversal of the Church's position. Probably the best way is to support those American Catholics who already realize that opposition to birth control is automatically support for increased misery and death. If such a reversal can be obtained, mankind's chances for survival will improve somewhat, and millions upon millions of Catholics will be able to lead better lives. But the population problem will not be "solved."

Biologists must promote understanding of the facts of reproductive biology which relate to matters of abortion and contraception. They must do more than simply reiterate the facts of population dynamics. They must point out the biological absurdity of equating a zygote (the cell created by joining of sperm and egg) or fetus (unborn child) with a human being. As Professor Garrett Hardin of the University of California pointed out, that is like confusing a set of blueprints with a building.[48] People are people because of the interaction of genetic information (stored in a chemical language) with an environment. Clearly, the most "humanizing" element of that environment is the cultural element, to which the child is not exposed until after birth. When conception is prevented or a fetus destroyed, the *potential* for another human being is lost, but that is all. That potential is lost *regardless* of the reason that conception does not occur—there is no biological difference if the egg is not fertilized because of timing or because of mechanical or other interference.

Biologists must point out that contraception is for many reasons more desirable than abortion. But they must also point out that in many cases abortion is much more desirable than childbirth. Above all, biologists must take the side of the hungry billions of *living* human beings today and tomorrow, not the side of *potential* human beings. Remember, unless, their numbers are limited, if those potential human beings are born, they will at best lead miserable lives and die young. We cannot permit the destruction of humanity to be abetted by a doctrine conceived in total ignorance of the biological facts of life.

Basically, I think the Catholic situation is much more amenable to solution than that associated with our current views of economics. The winds of change are clearly blowing in religion—blowing too late, perhaps, but blowing. Yet the idea of an ever-expanding economy fueled by population growth seems tightly entrenched in the minds of businessmen, if not in the minds of economists. Every new baby is viewed as a consumer to stimulate an ever-growing economy. Each baby is, of course, potentially one of the unemployed, but a consumer nonetheless. The Rienows[49] estimate that each American baby will consume in a 70-year life span, directly or indirectly: 26 million gallons of water, 21 thousand gallons of gasoline, 10 thousand pounds of meat, 28 thousand pounds of milk and cream, $5,000 to $8,000 in school building materials, $6,300 worth of clothing, and $7,000 worth of furniture. It's not a baby, it's Superconsumer!

Our entire economy is geared to growing population and monumental waste. Buy land and hold it; the price is sure to go up. Why? Exploding population on a finite planet. Buy natural resources stocks; their price is sure to go up. Why? Exploding population and finite resources. Buy automotive or airline stocks; their price is sure to go up. Why? More people to move around. Buy baby food stocks; their price is sure to go up. Why? You guess. And so it goes. Up goes the population and up goes that magical figure, the Gross National Product (GNP). And, as anyone who takes a close look at the glut, waste, pollution, and ugliness of America today can testify, it is well-named—as *gross* a product as one could wish for. We have assumed the role of the robber barons of all time. We have decided that we are the chosen people to steal all we can get of our planet's gradually stored and limited resources. To hell with future generations, and to hell with our fellow human beings today! We'll fly high now—hopefully they'll pay later.

We thought the game would end only in hundreds or even thousands of years through resource depletion. But the bill is coming due before we expected it. Now we find that may be among the least of our problems. The poor of the world show signs of not being happy with our position. Even the poor at home seem a little ill-disposed toward our behavior. Whether we can keep our position is open to question. But what has been properly called "the *effluent* society" shows signs of strangling itself without the intervention of enraged "have-nots." Will our gross national product soon be reduced to no national product?

The answer is that it surely will unless we take a hard

look at our present economic system. There are some very distinguished economists who do not feel that our capitalist system must be fueled by an ever-growing population or ever-continuing depletion of resources (both of which are impossible, anyway). There, in fact, seems to be no reason why the GNP cannot be kept growing for a very long time *without population growth.*

Dr. J. J. Spengler wrote,[50] "In the future, economic growth will depend mainly upon invention, innovation, technical progress, and capital formation, upon institutionalized growth-favoring arrangements. Population growth will probably play an even smaller role than I have assigned it in earlier discussion. *It is high time, therefore, that business cease looking upon the stork as a bird of good omen."* (My emphasis.)

Ways must be found to promote the idea that problems associated with population growth will more than cancel the "advantages" of financial prosperity. Perhaps the best way to do this would be to encourage Americans to ask exactly what our financial prosperity is for. What will be done with leisure time and money when all vacation spots are crowded beyond belief? Is it worth living in the Los Angeles smog for 50 weeks in order to spend two weeks in Yosemite Valley—when the Valley in the summer may be even more crowded than L.A. and twice as smoggy? What good is having the money for a fishing trip when fish are dead or poisonous because of pesticide pollution? Why own a fancy car in which to get asphyxiated in monster traffic jams? Do we want more and more of the same until we have destroyed ourselves? Sizable segments of our population, especially the young, are already answering that question: "Hell, no!" Their response should be carefully considered by population-promoting tycoons.

Obviously, the problem of our deteriorating environment is tied in very closely with the overall economic problem. We must reverse the attitudes so beautifully exemplified by one of our giants of industry when he said that "the ability of a river to absorb sewage is one of our great natural resources and should be utilized to the utmost."[51] Legal steps must be taken, and taken fast, to see to it that polluters pay through the nose for their destructive acts. The old idea that industry could create the mess and then the taxpayers must clean it up has to go. The garbage produced by an industry is the responsibility of that industry. The government should not use other people's money to clean it up. Keep the government out of business. Let it play its proper role in a capitalistic society—seeing to it that all segments of private enterprise do business honestly, seeing to it that the interests of the fishing industry are not subordinated to those of the petrochemical industry, seeing to it that your right to swim in a public lake is not subordinated to the desire of a steel company to make an inflated profit.

The federal policeman against environmental deterioration must have the power to monitor adequately and to enforce stiff regulations. It must be carefully insulated against the forces that will quickly be aligned against it. It is going to cost industry money. It is going to cost municipalities money. It is going to hit a lot of us where it hurts. We will have to do without two gas-gulping monster cars per family. We will have to learn to get along with some insect damage in our produce. We will have to get along with much less fancy packaging of the goods we purchase. We may have to use cleansers that get our clothes something less than "whiter than white." We may have to be satisfied with slower coast-to-coast transportation. Such may be the cost of survival. Of course, we may also have to get along with less emphysema, less cancer, less heart disease, less noise, less filth, less crowding, less need to work long hours or "moonlight," less robbery, less assault, less murder, and less threat of war. The pace of life may slow down. We may have more fishing, more relaxing, more time to watch TV, more time to drink beer (served in bottles that *must* be returned).

The federal government—presumably the Environmental Protection Agency—should place extremely strict controls on the use of dangerous pesticides and encourage research on economically and ecologically more reasonable methods of control. We have barely scratched the surface in what can be done with biological controls, including ways of manipulating the genetics of pest populations. We do not know enough about the ways that chemical and biological controls might be integrated in ecologically intelligent ways. But perhaps the greatest service the EPA might perform right from its inception would be to expose the stupidity and futility of today's pesticide practices. Properly constituted, the EPA should have a strong complement of systems ecologists—ecologists who use the methods of operations research and systems analysis to evaluate complex ecological systems. As a foretaste of what the EPA might say, let me quote to you from a letter from Professor K. E. F. Watt of the University of California, one of today's outstanding systems ecologists:

". . . most control programs are set up without a threshold; that is, spray is used each season whether significant densities of pests are present or not. Thus, this is an example of a business providing the amazing spectacle of supporting an overhead which is not associated with a corresponding marginal increase in gross profit. It is this type of practice which has led many fruit orchard owners into such dire economic straits that they have had to sell their land for housing projects or factory sites.

"It is most important to point out to the public that a pest control program should have two consequences: (1) either plant or animal being attacked by the pests should be saved, and (2) there should be fewer pests in subsequent generations following treatment. The yardstick by which all control programs should be evaluated comes from those dramatically successful programs in which plants or animals were saved, and pests declined in density. You are aware of examples that provide this yardstick . . . the Florida screwworm study is a prize example. *By this criterion most pesticide projects have been failures.*" (My emphasis.)

The federal government, perhaps the EPA, should also be responsible for pushing legislation to stop the wasting of resources. It should move toward creating a vast waste recovery industry, an industry that might well make "trash" obsolete. Reusable containers might be required by law for virtually all products, as has been suggested by Dr. Athelstan Spilhaus.[52] He points out the necessity of controlling trash and pollutants at the source, stating, "Regardless of what any economist tells me, I'm convinced by the second law of thermodynamics that it must be cheaper to collect something at the source than to scrape it off the buildings, wash it out of the clothes, and so forth." There's that old, immutable law again. If the product is deteriorated and scattered, usable energy has been lost, and more must be injected into the system if order is to be restored, by either collecting or reconstituting the product. The less deterioration or scattering we permit, the less energy we must use. Equally, products should be manufactured with a view to recycling the materials they are made from. While it takes energy to collect and reconstitute materials in this way, less energy normally is required than if the product were being manufactured from raw materials which must first be mined and refined. At the same time, recycling would relieve pressure on the raw materials—themselves nonrenewable resources—which are being consumed at ever-increasing rates.

The EPA also should take a good hard look at our energy budget, especially at the rate at which we are expending our irreplaceable fossil fuels. It should evaluate carefully the possible role of atomic fission or fusion in replacing fossil fuels as an energy source. It should also evaluate hydroelectric power in relation to the other two. These sources cannot be considered in isolation. Atomic facilities must have their waste disposal problems integrated into the evaluation. Hydroelectric power must be considered in a framework of the gradual altering of the ecology of rivers and flood plains and of Earth's topography through the building and silting up of dams. It must be considered in relationship to salmon fisheries and downstream farming. Both atomic and hydroelectric power must be considered in relation to the expenditures of fossil fuels required to mine, transport, and process the metals and concrete from which facilities are built. That we are presently living beyond our means is obvious from the simple fact that we are madly depleting nonreplenishable resources. Careful plans must be laid for getting the Earth back in balance, on the hopeful assumption that some way can be found to avoid the doom now confronting us.

By now you are probably fed up with this discussion. Americans will do none of these things, you say. Well, I'm inclined to agree. As an eternal optimist, however, I will provide some suggestions in the last chapter of this book for what you might do to improve the chances that action will be taken. Improve them from, say, one in a thousand to one in a hundred, but improve them. Meanwhile let's make the unlikely assumption that this country will turn aside from its suicidal course and start a sensible domestic program of population and environmental control. How can we then help with the world problem?

Realism and International Aid

Once the United States has begun to adopt sane policies at home, we will be in a position to take the lead in finding a solution to the problem on a world scale. What we will need first and foremost is a plan that will produce a maximum amelioration of the time of famines with the relatively limited resources we have in hand. Even drastic population control measures need decades to work, and we do not have the capacity even to begin to feed the needy of the world. Our giant food surpluses are gone, and even at maximum production we would not be able to produce surplus enough for all (to say nothing of getting it properly distributed). In addition, we are the only country which is in a position to give away food. Canada, Australia, Argentina, and the other few countries with exportable surpluses will be largely occupied with selling food to hungry countries that are in a position to pay. These granary countries will need the income that they earn in this way, or the goods they can receive in exchange for food. The UDCs cannot expect major charity from them.

What kind of policies should we be designing to guide our actions during the time of famines? To my knowledge, there has been only one realistic suggestion in this area—a policy proposed by William and Paul Paddock in their book *Famine—1975!* The Paddocks suggest a

146

policy based on the concept of "triage" borrowed from military medicine. The idea briefly is this: When casualties crowd a dressing station to the point where all cannot be cared for by the limited medical staff, some decisions must be made on who will be treated. For this purpose the triage system of classification was developed. All incoming casualties are placed in one of three classes. In the first class are those who will die regardless of treatment. In the second class are those who will survive regardless of treatment. The third contains those who can be saved only if they are given prompt treatment. When medical aid is severely limited, it is concentrated only on the third group—the others are left untreated.

The Paddocks suggest that we devise a similar system for classifying nations. Some will undergo the transition to self-sufficiency without drastic aid from us. They will be ones with abundant money for foreign purchases, or with efficient governments, strong population control programs, and strong agricultural development programs. Although our aid might help them, they could get along without it. Some nations, on the other hand, may become self-sufficient if we give them help. They have a chance to make it if we can give them some food to tide them over. Finally there is the last tragic category —those countries that are so far behind in the population-food game that there is no hope that our food aid will see them through to self-sufficiency.

The Paddocks feel that our limited assistance should go to those whom it would save, not to those who can survive without it or those who can't be saved in any case. Their views have not, to say the least, been greeted with enthusiasm by foreign governments, by those in our government whose jobs depend on the willy-nilly spreading of American largesse abroad, or by the assorted do-gooders who are deeply involved in the apparatus of international food charity. Criticism from some of those groups is a compliment.

In my opinion, there is no rational choice *except* to adopt some form of Paddocks' strategy, at least as far as food distribution during famine is concerned. They deserve immense credit for their courage and foresight in publishing *Famine—1975!*, which may be remembered as one of the most important books of our age.

What might be a possible strategy leading to man's passage with minimum casualties through the next fateful decade or two? Obviously, if we are to find a long-range solution, the full resources of the United States and the other ODCs must be brought to bear. In the first edition of this book I suggested that the United States, Russia, Great Britain, Canada, Japan, Australia, Europe, and other ODCs immediately set up, through the United Nations, a machinery for "area rehabilitation." This plan involved simultaneous population control, agricultural development, and, where resources warrant it, industrialization of selected countries or sections of countries. The bedrock requirement of the program would have to be population control, necessarily including migration control to prevent swamping of aided areas by the less fortunate. Of course, the size of the areas covered would be dependent in no small part on the scale and effectiveness of the effort made by the ODCs. I had hoped that the United States could be persuaded to lead the way, even though our efforts toward aiding the UDCs, in terms of the percentage of our gross national product committed, have been behind that of many other ODCs, who could less well afford it.

Needless to say, in the three years since I proposed the plan, nothing whatever has occurred to indicate that the world community is willing to undertake anything remotely resembling it. We still face a three-part dilemma. First, even the most dramatic, all out, self-sacrificing efforts by the ODCs, with full cooperation from the

UDCs, would probably be insufficient to avoid massive calamity. Second, there is no sign of willingness for *any* level of self-sacrifice among the ODCs, and little indication that most UDCs would sit still for a world organization allocating aid. One suspects, for instance, that many dictators in UDCs might prefer their people to starve rather than to submit to land reforms and other policies which might be the requirements for aid (since the U.N. could not legitimately funnel aid into the pockets of ruling oligarchies). And third, although the people of the ODCs are unwilling even to consider an adequate program of aid, many of them think it "immoral" to allocate inadequate aid in such a way as to do the most good. Such "moralists" attack the Paddocks instead of attacking a society which fights obesity while millions starve.

If we could, somehow, get a program underway in which the ODCs made a genuine attempt to aid the UDCs, what form might that program take? The specific requirements of the program would vary from area to area. Possibly the first step in all areas would be to set up relay stations and distribute small transistorized TV sets to villages for communal viewing of satellite-transmitted programs. We must have channels for reaching the largely rural populations of the "other world." TV programs would explain the rehabilitation plan for each area. These programs would have to be produced with the combined skills of people with great expertise in the subjects to be presented and intimate knowledge of the target population. The programs could be presented both "straight" and as "entertainment." They would introduce the UDC populations to such things as the need for agricultural innovations and public health measures. The programs would use the prospect of increased affluence as a major incentive for gaining cooperation. It seems unlikely that the threat of future starvation would have much impact. If necessary, however, the TV channel could be used to make it clear that the continuance of food supplies depends on the co-operation of the people in the area. Perhaps they could be made to realize that only by making progress toward population control and self-sufficiency can they avoid disaster.

Other steps would vary a great deal from place to place. In some agricultural areas needs would be well enough known for assistance to start immediately, perhaps with "on site" training of agricultural technicians. Such a program could lead to a sort of "county agricultural agent" system in which trained people work closely with farmers. These systems have proved their great worth in many parts of the world. Schools to train agents and other agricultural personnel, including farmers brought in on rotation, would be of immense value to the agriculture of most UDCs.

In some places the problems of agriculture might be so severe that research stations might have to function for a decade or so before local agriculture had a chance of being revolutionized. "Improved" strains of various crops developed elsewhere might not grow satisfactorily or might be unacceptable to the local people as food. Since the supply of trained people suitable for running stations doing research in tropical and semitropical agriculture is limited, priority systems for station establishment must be set up. At the same time, ways must be found to increase the supply of agricultural scientists being trained—both in ODCs and UDCs.

In all areas studies should be initiated to determine how much agricultural and industrial development is feasible. It must be determined how many people, at each stage of development, can live reasonably comfortable, secure lives in each area. That is, demographic goals must be set that are reasonable in the light of each country's and the world's basic resources. Unless demographic goals are set and met, the entire program will inevitably fail. Population control must be made to work, or all our other efforts will have been in vain.

Needless to say, the sociopolitical problems of initiating such a program would be colossal. It might not, for instance, be feasible to operate through the United Nations, because it will be impossible to aid all countries equally. This problem might be sidestepped by using the "area" concept rather than strictly political units. Thus, if migration could be controlled, some sections of India might be aided and others not. It might be to mankind's advantage to have some UDCs more divided or even re-arranged, especially along economic axes. After all, most political boundaries in Southern Asia and Africa reflect, not economically viable units, but the conflicting interests of European powers 75 years ago. I know this all sounds very callous, but remember the alternative. The callous acts have long since been committed by those who over the years have obstructed a birth rate solution or downgraded or ignored the entire problem. The callous acts are those of the Western world designed to keep the majority of humanity in the role of impoverished suppliers of raw materials. Now the time has come to pay the piper, and the same kind of obstructionists remain. If they succeed, we will all go down the drain.

While we are working toward setting up a world program of the general sort outlined above, the United States could take effective unilateral action in many cases. A good example of how we might have acted can be built around the Chandrasekhar incident I mentioned earlier. When we suggested sterilizing all Indian males with three or more children, he should have encouraged the Indian government to go ahead with the plan. We should have volunteered logistic support in the form of helicopters, vehicles, and surgical instruments. We should have sent doctors to aid in the program by setting up centers for training para-medical personnel to do vasectomies. Coercion? Perhaps, but coercion in a good cause. I am sometimes astounded at the attitudes of Americans who are horrified at the prospect of our government insisting on population control as the price of food aid. All too often the very same people are fully in support of applying military force against those who disagree with our form of government or our rapacious foreign policy. We must be just as relentless in pushing for population control around the world, together with rearrangement of trade relations to benefit UDCs, and massive economic aid.

I wish I could offer you some sugarcoated solutions, but I'm afraid the time for them is long gone. A cancer is an uncontrolled multiplication of cells; the population explosion is an uncontrolled multiplication of people. Treating only the symptoms of cancer may make the victim more comfortable at first, but eventually he dies —often horribly. A similar fate awaits a world with a population explosion if only the symptoms are treated. We must shift our efforts from treatment of the symptoms to the cutting out of the cancer. The operation will demand many apparently brutal and heartless decisions. The pain may be intense. But the disease is so far advanced that only with radical surgery does the patient have a chance of survival.

So far I have talked primarily about the strategy for easing us through the hazardous times just ahead. But what of our ultimate goals? That, of course, is something that needs a great deal of discussion in the United States and elsewhere. Obviously, we need a stable world population with its size rationally controlled by society. But what should the size of that population be? What is the optimum number of human beings that the Earth can support? What are the limiting factors for humanity, and at what level does each one limit us? These are extremely complex questions. They involve value judgments about how crowded we should be. They also include technical questions of how crowded we *can* be. Research should obviously be initiated in both areas immediately.

If we are to decide how crowded we should be, we must know a great deal more about man's perception of crowding and about how crowding affects human beings. Certainly people in different cultures and subcultures have different views of what densities of people (people per unit area) constitute crowding under differing conditions. But what exactly are those densities and conditions? Under what conditions do people consider themselves neither crowded nor lonely? Research on these questions has barely been started. It must be accompanied by studies of how crowding affects people, including both "overcrowding" and "undercrowding." These problems are more difficult to study, especially since the effects of crowding are often confounded by poverty, poor diet, unattractive surroundings, and other related phenomena.

But, difficult as these problems are, they must be investigated. We know all too well that when rats or other animals are overcrowded, the results are pronounced and usually unpleasant. Social systems may break down, cannibalism may occur, breeding may cease altogether. The results may not bode well for human beings as they get more and more crowded. But extrapolating from the behavior of rats to the behavior of human beings is much more risky than extrapolating from the physiology of rats to the physiology of human beings. Man's physical characteristics are much more ratlike than are his social systems.

Experimental work with human beings conducted at Stanford and Columbia universities has just begun, but it has come up with some interesting results. Crowding alone, at least for periods of a few hours, seems to have no effect upon people's work performance, whether it is a routine task or a much more complex one requiring concentration. However, crowding does seem to increase hostility among men, although not among women.

Crowding reduces hostility in mixed groups! These findings have interesting implications for numerous human situations and problems, from the sexual makeup of juries and decision-making bodies to the design of housing and offices to the origins of antisocial behavior. But these preliminary experiments with human beings and studies of human behavior in cities make it seem unlikely that pathological effects of crowding alone will limit the human population. Shortage of food, for instance, will limit us long before the density of the world population approaches those densities now found in many large cities where people are still merrily overbreeding!

Within the limits imposed by nature, I would view an optimum population size for the Earth to be one permitting any individual to be as crowded or as alone as he or she wished. Enough people should be present so that large cities are possible, but people should not be so numerous as to prevent people who so desire from being hermits. Pretty idealistic, but not impossible in theory. Besides, some very far-reaching changes are going to be required in human society over the next few decades, regardless of whether or not we stop the population explosion. We've already reached a population size relative to our resources at which many of our institutions no longer function properly. As the distinguished historian, Walter Prescott Webb, pointed out 19 years ago,[53] with the closing of the World Frontier, a set of basic institutions and attitudes became outdated. When the Western Hemisphere was opened to exploitation by Europeans, a crowded condition suddenly was converted into an uncrowded one. In 1500 the ratio of people to available land in Europe was estimated to have been about 27 people per square mile. The addition of the vast, virtually unpopulated frontier of the New World moved this ratio back down to less than five per square mile. As Webb said, the frontier was, in

essence, "a vast body of wealth without proprietors."
Europeans moved rapidly to exploit the spatial, mineral,
and other material wealth of the New World. They
created an unprecedented economic boom that lasted
some 400 years. The boom is clearly over, however, at
least as far as land is concerned. The man/land ratio
went beyond 27 people per square mile again before
1930. Since all of the material things on which the boom
depended also come ultimately from the land, the entire boom is also clearly limited. Of course, how to end
that boom gracefully, without the most fantastic "bust"
of all time, is what this book is all about.

Somehow we've got to change from a growth-orient-
ed, exploitative system to one focused on stability and
conservation. Our entire system of orienting to nature
must undergo a revolution. And that revolution is going
to be extremely difficult to pull off, since the attitudes
of Western culture toward nature are deeply rooted in
Judeo-Christian tradition. Unlike people in many other
cultures, we see man's basic role as that of dominating
nature, rather than as living in harmony with it. This
entire problem has been elegantly discussed by Professor Lynn White, Jr., in *Science* magazine.[54] He points
out, for instance, that before the Christian era trees,
springs, hills, streams, and other objects of nature had
guardian spirits. These spirits had to be approached and
placated before one could safely invade their territory.
As White says, "By destroying pagan animism, Chris-
tianity made it possible to exploit nature in a mood of
indifference to the feelings of natural objects." Chris-
tianity fostered the wide spread of basic ideas of "progress" and of time as something linear, nonrepeating,
and absolute, flowing from the future into the past. Such
ideas were foreign to the Greeks and Romans, who had
a cyclical (repeating) view of time and could not en-
vision the world as having a beginning. Although a
modern physicist's view of time might be somewhat

closer to that of the Greeks than the Christians, it is obvious that the Christian view is the one held by most of us. God designed and started the whole business for our benefit. He made a world for us to dominate and exploit. Our European ancestors had long since developed the "proper" attitudes when the opportunity to exploit the New World appeared.

Both science and technology can clearly be seen to have their historical roots in natural theology and the Christian dogma of man's rightful mastery over nature. Therefore, as White claims, it is probably in vain that so many look to science and technology to solve our present ecological crisis. Much more basic changes are needed, perhaps of the type exemplified by the much-despised "hippie" movement—a movement that adopts most of its religious ideas from the non-Christian East. It is a movement wrapped up in Zen Buddhism, love, and a disdain for material wealth. It is small wonder that our society is horrified at hippies' behavior—it goes against our most cherished ethical ideas. I think it would be well if those of us who are totally ensnared in the non-hip part of our culture paid a great deal of attention to the movement, rather than condemn it out of hand. They may not have *the* answer, but they may have *an* answer. At the very least they are asking the proper questions. Here is what White, a churchman, has to say: "Both our present science and our present technology are so tinctured with orthodox Christian arrogance toward nature that no solution for our ecologic crisis can be expected from them alone. Since the roots of our trouble are so largely religious, the remedy must also be essentially religious, whether we call it that or not."

So there is considerable reason for believing that extremely fundamental changes in our society are going to be required in order to preserve any semblance of the world we know. Furthermore, those changes are going to have to take place in a framework of certain natural limits. For, as I hope I have convinced you, even though we would like to dominate nature, it still dominates us!

What are those limits that are imposed by nature? We don't know exactly. Finding out will involve complex questions of energy sources and the availability of the materials necessary for the production of food. There is some disagreement as to exactly how dependent upon fossil fuels we shall remain and what the ultimate consequences of their depletion beyond certain levels will be. But at a minimum it seems safe to say that a population of one billion people could be sustained in reasonable comfort for perhaps 1,000 years if resources were husbanded carefully. A mere century of stability should provide ample time to investigate most technological leads and to do the social adjusting and policy planning necessary to set realistic goals on a more or less permanent basis. Our big problem for the next century is to bring the population under control, then to reduce its size to a supportable level, while creating an atmosphere in which necessary changes, investigations, and planning can take place. If we are not successful in reducing the population size to that low level, but do stabilize it at perhaps four or five billion, we will still have a chance. Of course, mankind's options will be fewer and people's lives certainly less pleasant than if the lower figure were attained.

The Chances of Success

Many of you are doubtless saying now, "It's too un-realistic—it can't be done." I think you're probably right—as I said earlier, the chances of success are small. Indeed, they are probably infinitesimal, if success is to be measured only by the initiation of a complete program such as I have suggested. But partial programs can help. Indeed, even if the worst happens, short of the end of civilization, efforts toward solving the population problem may not be in vain. Suppose we do not prevent massive famines. Suppose there are widespread plagues. Suppose a billion people perish. At least if we have called enough attention to the problem, we may be able to avoid a repetition of the whole mess. We must make it impossible for people to blame the calamity on too little food or technological failures or "acts of God." They must at least face the essential cause of the problem—overpopulation.

Chapter 5
WHAT CAN YOU DO?

The question I am most frequently asked after giving talks about the population explosion is, "What can I do to help?" The obvious first answer is, "Set an example—don't have more than two children." That reply really sets the pace, because I am becoming more and more convinced that the only real hope in this crisis lies in the grass-roots activities of individuals. We must change public opinion in this country, and through public opinion change the direction of our government. The fact that we cannot count on vast funds to support our efforts does not have to be an insurmountable obstacle. In the eight years that I have been a part-time propagandist, I have found that many people in influential positions share my concern. I have had encouraging letters from all over the world. People in radio and television have been extremely helpful in providing exposure for the issues. Exposure for the issues, however, is not enough. We must create enough pressure to convince politicians that their political survival is at stake unless they get behind some really effective measures to deal with mankind's most pressing problem. Now for some concrete suggestions of what you can do.

Join ZPG

First of all, get together with people who share your concerns. It's easier, pleasanter and generally more effective to crusade in a group. Zero Population Growth, Inc., is a nonprofit organization dedicated to bringing population size under control. It had about 30,000 members in early 1971 and was growing rapidly. Write to ZPG, 330 Second Street, Los Altos, California 94022, the national headquarters; it will tell you about your local chapter.

Write Letters

Do not underestimate the power of the letter in the eyes of politicians and others in positions of power. Just think of the effect on our politics if every Senator and Representative received 100 different, intelligent letters every day, demanding action on the population explosion. In case you don't know who your Senators are or who your Representative is, you can find out by calling your public library. Sample letters to a Senator and a Representative are included in the Appendix. Do not, of course, copy these. Make up your own, based on this book or on some of those listed in the bibliography. Try to confine your comments to a single page. For your convenience, here is a brief checklist of points you might want to make:

1. Population is far outstripping food production.
2. More than half of the world is hungry; many are dying of starvation.
3. Population growth must come to an end.
4. Our only choices are a lower birth rate or a bigger death rate.
5. Long-term growth rate must be zero.
6. It is necessary to plan for a stable population of optimum size.

7. Family planning alone does not lead to population control.

8. Change of attitudes is more important than contraceptive technology in population control.

9. Need for better contraceptive methods is great, notwithstanding (8).

10. In short term the only feasible way to increase food production greatly is by increasing yield on land already under production.

11. Research in tropical ecology and agriculture is badly needed.

12. A firm agricultural base is a prerequisite for industrialization.

13. Not all countries can be industrialized.

14. ODCs cannot feed UDCs.

15. Environmental deterioration poses a colossal threat to man's survival.

16. The world is running short of vital resources, and the American economic system must adjust to this reality.

17. Government attention to this entire problem has been insignificant in proportion to the seriousness of the situation.

Obviously even the above list covers more points than one could reasonably make in a single letter. Try to develop a few of them and use follow-up letters to develop others. Try to connect letters to politicians with local projects and problems in which you know they are interested. If they come from the shores of the Great Lakes, mention the role population pressures are playing in the destruction of those lakes. If they come from Los Angeles, point out that the smog may be caused by too many cars, but that too many cars are caused by too many people. If the politicians you address are concerned with conservation, point out that conservation is a losing game without population control. Above all, when you write to a legislator about population-environment matters ask him *to tell you what his stands are.* Require an answer, and keep after him until you get it. As a congressman once told me, "Hold his feet to the fire." Be specific. "How would you vote on a bill to provide every American woman with access to subsidized abortion on demand? Why?" "Why did you vote against the International Survival Tax bill?" When you get an answer, you can tell him why you approve or disapprove of his position.

Letters may, of course, be written to state and local officials as well. These, too, would best focus on local issues. If a member of a local government is opposing needed bonds, point out that his efforts would be more socially constructive if he were promoting population control. Fewer kids require fewer schools. If a state representative wants to destroy a park in order to build a freeway, point out that, if he had promoted population control in the past, the freeway might be unnecessary. Bombard with mail any elected official who opposes liberalizing abortion laws.

Editors of magazines and newspapers are excellent targets for letters. Complain bitterly about any positive treatment of large families. Attack the publicizing of "mothers of the year" unless they have no more than two children or have adopted the extra ones. Request that the publications you address stop carrying any advertising implying by statement or inference that it is socially acceptable to have more than two children. Point out that any promotion of the idea that a growing population means prosperity is making a contribution to the destruction of America. Television and radio stations should be subjected to similar constant pressure. Series featuring large families should be assailed. More programming about the population crisis should be demanded. Ask for prime time programs on sex education and the use of contraceptives. Raise a fuss whenever programming or commercials promote reproductive irresponsibility. Ask for programs that expose our disgraceful laws regulating abortion and contraception. A letter to a television station is included in the Appendix as one example of what you might write.

Another target for your letters is the business community, including chambers of commerce. Those producing offensive advertisements or advertising during offensive television programs should be threatened with boycott. Be tough: "Dear Sir: Your company's advertisement was shown in the middle of *The Saturday Family,* implying your sponsorship of that program. The day is upon us when we can no longer tolerate television programs that feature large families as if they still represented acceptable behavior on the part of parents. I will never buy another of your franistans until . . ." Chambers of commerce are especially "black hat" on matters of population, and should be called down whenever they step out of line.

Finally, if you are a Catholic, you should let your Church know that you strongly disapprove of its policies on birth control. You can withdraw your financial support from the diocese and channel it into liberal Catholic causes. Remember that any organized religion is also a political organization and therefore responsive to grassroots pressure. The Church has survived for almost two millenna by adjusting, under pressure, to the times. You can help it survive by pressuring it to change. Indeed, if you belong to any religious or charitable organization that has as one goal the treatment of the symptoms of overpopulation, you should make it clear to the organization that its policies are not geared to realities. Examples of two responsible Catholics' approaches to their Church are given in the Appendix, along with a letter written by a Lutheran to the head of his Church.

You can surely think of other people to whom writing such letters would be helpful. Above all, if you really want to survive, start writing! Just think, if only 30,000 concerned people wrote one letter a day, the Establishment would be inundated with ten million letters a year. It will take effort and tenacity. But consider what will happen if we don't do it!

Organize Action Groups

If ZPG does not have a chapter in your area, organize one. The time has come for us to assemble groups of dedicated people who do not want to see our way of life destroyed by the population explosion. Feel lonely while writing your letter-a-day? Get a few chapter members together and hold a letter-writing party once a week. Develop a blacklist of people, companies, and organizations impeding population control or promoting environmental deterioration and go to work on them. Organize boycotts of products of guilty companies. Work for the opponents of guilty politicians. Help each other write speeches and have the most vocal members of your chapter present them at PTAs, service clubs, or anywhere else you can get an audience. Telephone in to "talk shows" on radio or television and start discussions on population control. If sex education in your school system is inadequate (it is in almost all), educate yourself and start classes for the children in your group. Give your child an IUD to take to "show and tell." Above all, *raise a stink.* Let other people know how serious your group thinks the problem is and how determined you are to do something about it.

How much can be accomplished by your chapter will depend a great deal on how much enthusiasm for action you can generate and maintain. Some difficulty will be encountered in disagreement over exact steps to be taken, but if your goal is kept clearly in mind, this should be minimal.

Positive Reinforcement

So far I've concentrated on the attack. A great deal of good can be done by encouraging those who are moving in the right direction. People like Senator Packwood and Mr. Rickelshaus of the EPA like to know that their efforts are appreciated, too. If a politician makes a sensible statement on population or environmental problems, write him immediately and praise him, and if he represents you, assure him of your vote. If he takes a strong stand on the problem, do volunteer work for him. Help him get reelected by a landslide. Of course, the same goes for business as a whole and the communications industry in general. When they move in the right direction, let them hear about it. If a beer company pays a reward for returning empty cans, switch to that brand—and write the president of the company to tell him you're doing it. When a TV or radio show points up the problems of overpopulation, write a letter of thanks to the station. Johnny Carson and Arthur Godfrey have been outstanding in furthering public knowledge of the population problem. Let them hear from you.

Proselytize Friends and Associates

At no small risk of being considered a nut, you can do a lot of good by persuading your personal acquaintances that the crisis is here, that something must be done, and that they can help. What follows are some specific suggestions for arguments that may help in certain circumstances. They are classified on the basis of a target individual.

TARGET ALREADY HAS EIGHT KIDS. Emphasize that the need for family limitation was not obvious before. Point out that target surely would not behave that way today. Target should now encourage others to "do as I say," not "do as I did." Remind him that if his children follow his example, he'll have 64 grandchildren to buy Christmas and birthday presents for.

TARGET IS CHILDLESS. Emphasize that target is paying through the nose to raise other people's children. Praise target for selfless devotion to mankind (even if you suspect target is sterile). Target should encourage others to "do as I do."

TARGET HAS TWO CHILDREN. Suggest that two is plenty. If more are desired, suggest adoption. Point out that if target really loves children, more good can be done by adopting a child who has already been born.

Target will have the pleasure of rearing the child, the child will have a good home. If target decides to have further children, suggest that target is doing it for personal satisfaction, not out of love of children.

TARGET IS EXTREME CONSERVATIVE. Point out that overpopulation breeds conditions in which communism and "big government" thrive. Explain that larger numbers weaken, not strengthen, the United States. Report that China and other Communist countries have realized this and are moving to limit their populations. Remind target that the United States fought World War II with a population of less than 150 million people, and that future wars will depend more on firepower than manpower.

TARGET IS EXTREME LIBERAL. Emphasize that the rich are getting richer and the poor poorer, both in the United States and in the world as a whole. Declare that as long as population continues to grow, this disparity will worsen, and the goal of a "fair deal" for all will recede.

TARGET IS A DEEPLY RELIGIOUS CATHOLIC. Cite support of religious leaders of *all* faiths for the need to limit populations. Point out that it is mainly a question of technique of birth control that divides the Catholic Church today. Show target Dr. Thomas's statement in Chapter IV and his letter and that of Dr. Parnell in the appendix to indicate how informed Catholic opinion differs with the hierarchy. Quote to target from Dr. M. H. Mothersill's book *Birth Control and Conscience*: "There are religious leaders today in the twentieth century who strain at the gnat of artificial contraception and then swallow the camel of overpopulation, poverty, famine, crime, and the conditions which lead to war. Then they say, 'Peace, Peace!' when by their outdated pro-nationalism they have induced conditions such that there can be no peace!"

TARGET SAYS THERE IS AN "INALIENABLE RIGHT" TO HAVE AS MANY CHILDREN AS ONE WANTS. Point out that as long as the invention of inalienable rights is in vogue, you've invented a few of your own. They are:

1. The right to limit our families.
2. The right to eat.
3. The right to eat meat.
4. The right to drink pure water.
5. The right to live uncrowded in decent homes.
6. The right to avoid regimentation.
7. The right to hunt and fish.
8. The right to view natural beauty.
9. The right to breathe clean air.
10. The right to silence.
11. The right to avoid pesticide poisoning.
12. The right to be free of thermonuclear war.
13. The right to educate our children.
14. The right to have grandchildren.
15. The right to have great-grandchildren.

Since the price of having all these "inalienable rights" is giving up the right to irresponsible reproduction, you win 15 "rights" to one.

TARGET BRINGS UP QUESTIONS OF EUGENICS— SHOULDN'T SOME PEOPLE BREED AND OTHERS BE STERILIZED? This is an old routine—basically target is saying, "My superior kind should breed, yours should abstain for the good of mankind." Some targets may be concerned, for instance, with possible degeneration of human intelligence to overbreeding of the "less smart." Quote me as a specialist on genetic changes in populations to the effect that:

1. Intelligence in man has both genetic and environmental components. You might think of each individual as having an inherited possible range of intelligence. His or her environment—diet, home life, schooling—determine what level within that range is

actually achieved. This is an oversimplification, but it is close enough.

2. If, over perhaps five generations, those at the lower end of the genetic intelligence scale far outbred those at the upper end, the average I.Q. in the population could be expected to be reduced by a few points.

3. If such a change were detected, average I.Q. could be returned to its previous level by the proper breeding program—that is, the change would be reversible.

4. There is no evidence that any such drastic differential in breeding exists.

5. It is critical that we start reducing the number of people in this generation—worrying about genetic effects over the next four to five generations would be pointless even if we could detect a differential today.

6. Anyone really concerned with raising the level of intelligence in our population should fight to raise the environmental component. We *know* that drastic increases can be made in one generation by improved home and school situations and in some cases by improved diet.

7. Most geneticists feel that if the genetic component of human intelligence is to be manipulated in the future, it is likely to be dealt with biochemically by treating individuals. Huge selective breeding programs on populations present many technical, social, and political difficulties.

8. Research *is* being done on the estimation of the genetic component of variance in quantitative characters like intelligence, but to date we have not come close to solving the genetic problems of determining an individual's intellectual endowment. Even more importantly, we have not solved the problems of cross-cultural I.Q. testing. When we can do those things, we will easily be able to ask the question whether tall people are genetically smarter than short

WHAT CAN YOU DO? 173

people, or whether black people may be smarter than white people. The results would be of some very limited academic interest to biologists and sociologists. For instance, environmental deprivation may have created strong selection for genetic intelligence in black populations, so that the average genetic I.Q. of Negroes might be a few points higher than that of the white population. It is clear from evidence on other similar genetic characters that no two samples of *Homo sapiens* would be identical with respect to genetic intelligence. A sample of Swedes would differ from a sample of Englishmen. A sample of carpenters would differ from a sample of plumbers. Tall people would differ from short people, and two different samples of tall Anglo-Saxon Protestants would differ from each other. It is also clear that any social action on genetic intelligence would be taken on the basis of that characteristic in an individual, and not on the basis of height, eye color, skin color, tooth size, blood type, or the like. For instance, once you knew each child's genetic intelligence, you would use that information, not skin color or hair type, to judge his or her educational potential. Thus the claim that studies of genetic I.Q. in a context of skin color are biologically or sociologically important is absolute and utter nonsense. Clearly, the genetic quality question is a red herring and should be kept out of our action program for the next generation.

TARGET IS A MEMBER OF A MINORITY GROUP. This target may very well feel that "population control" is aimed at blacks and other minorities—a form of genocide, the militants call it. Unhappily, enough people talking about population control do think it should be applied to other groups to justify this fear. These individuals often have the idea that the population explosion is caused by "other people," not themselves. Or they may think that it is a problem only of UDCs.

Nothing could be further from the truth. In the U. S., the great majority of births, including unwanted births, occur among the middle and affluent classes. Moreover, it is the behavior of these same groups which causes the greatest symptom of overpopulation in the U. S.—environmental deterioration. Minority groups usually are the prime victims of this and related symptoms, such as unemployment and rising crime rates. And until recently, the poor were largely denied even the means to limit their families. If first responsibility to reduce birth rates rests with any one group in the U. S. it rests with the affluent.

Hopefully, if the nonpoor, white segments of the population establish population control among themselves, the poor and the minorities will realize that their futures are as much at stake as everyone else's. This is the only way that the genocide accusation can be defused. Remember ZPG's motto: "The population bomb is everyone's baby."

TARGET IS UNIVERSITY PROFESSOR. Chances are your target will be intellectually convinced that there is a problem. In all probability, however, he will be unable to take action because his training and current environment all militate *against* action. His idea of "action" is to form a committee or to urge "more research." Both courses are actually substitutes for action. Neither will do much good in the crisis we face now. We've got lots of committees, and decades ago enough research had been done at least to outline the problem and make clear many of the steps necessary to solve it. Unless those steps are taken, research initiated today will be terminated not by success but by the problem under investigation. It is unwise for people in the woods downwind from a roaring forest fire to sit down and start research on new methods of fire fighting or on techniques of reforestation—unless a very able and adequate crew is

WHAT CAN YOU DO? 175

already combating the blaze with whatever methods are already available.

You must convince the professor that he should immediately use his influence in every way possible within and outside of the university to get the fire crews on the line. The population crisis must be an integral part of his teaching—it is pertinent to *every* subject. He must use the prestige of his position in writing letters to whomever he thinks he can influence most. If he is in English or drama, he may be able to write novels or plays emphasizing near-future worlds in which famines or plagues are changing the very nature of mankind and his societies. If he is in economics or business school, he can "hit the road" lecturing to business groups and industrial conferences on "The Stork as an Enemy of Capitalism." If he is in the physical sciences, he can write strong letters to his narrow-minded colleagues who are proposing idiotic panaceas to solve the food problem. Any scientist can be urged to write to the *Scientific American* and similar journals to ask the editors to stop accepting ecopornography or advertisements that imply that a technology for mining or farming the sea can save humanity. The high standards that these journals maintain in their articles should also apply to their advertising. Scientists who serve on government committees can be pressed to exploit their position to prod our slow-moving government. Any professor, lecturing anywhere, can at least insert into his lecture a "commercial" on the problem: "And so I come to the end of my discussion of the literary significance of Darwin's hangnail. In conclusion, I would like to remind you that our Society for the Study of Darwin's Hangnail can only exist in a world in which there is leisure time for intellectual pursuits, and a social system which permits such pursuits. Unless something is done *now* to bring the runaway human population under control, the SSDH will not long endure."

Within his university, the professor can be urged to help pave the way for the momentous changes that are certain to rock society and the medieval structure of his institution as the population explosion comes to a halt. Whatever stops the explosion, it is clear that today's deteriorating educational system will be shaken from top to bottom. Universities are already under assault from politicians. They are facing a wave of ideas and protests from students and open attack from political radicals. If we survive the crisis, new methods of teaching are in most cases going to replace the 50-minute lecture. New subjects are being added now, so there will be a strong trend toward deleting many old ones. Patchwork departmental structures will go, as will much of today's emphasis on tests and grading. *If* we get through the crisis, universities will evolve or die. But before we can find out which, we must first get through the crisis.

TARGET IS A SCHOOLTEACHER. It will be easy for you to convince most schoolteachers that the population problem is *very real*. They have been struggling with overcrowded classrooms and ghetto children for a long time. They see first-hand the inability of our society to provide a proper environment for its major product—children. Recommending action to schoolteachers is another problem. They are under the thumb of school boards that all too often are opposed to the teaching of anything socially important in school. Race relations, sex, politics, religion may all be "too controversial." Those subjects should be "taught at home." The parents of the children are, of course, usually hopelessly incompetent to teach any of these subjects. Why shouldn't they be? After all, they were educated by the very same school system. But this doesn't bother the school boards. They were never taught to think through a problem. They had reading, writing, arithmetic, and social studies just like Grandpa. Between the teacher and the school board stand the school administrators. The motto of most school administrators is simple: "Don't make waves."

So unless your teacher friend is one of the fortunate few in really first-rate educational systems or institutions, any determined public action inside or outside of school may just cost him his job. Subtle propaganda to the kiddies and letter writing may be all you can ask for. But do ask for that.

TARGET IS A "DOVE." A very large segment of our population is deeply committed to an antiwar stance, as well they should be. But they are to some extent concentrating on just one more symptom of the disease of overpopulation. Population pressures promote wars, whether the pressures are real or simply imagined. When Pope Urban II preached the First Crusade in November, 1095, he referred to the advantages of gaining new lands. Indeed, as Professor D. L. Bilderback, a historian at Fresno State College, has pointed out, the "First Crusade was made up largely of second sons who were dispossessed by the increasing European attachment to primogeniture (inheritance by the first-born son)." There is also evidence of considerable effort in 15th-century Europe in activities such as land reclamation. Things seem to have been getting pretty crowded and difficult for Europeans just before the opening of the New World frontier. Needless to say, the expanding, exploiting swarms of Europeans fought wars, not only among themselves, but against the small native populations, as they scrambled over the newly available territories.

In more recent history we have the stunning example of Nazi Germany's drive for "Lebensraum" (territory for expansion) and Japan's attempt to relieve the crowded condition of her small islands. Whether or not things were really all that difficult for the Germans is a point for debate. Germany is probably in worse shape for land today than she was in 1935. but the Bonn government does not promote this as a problem. Nonetheless Professor Bilderback feels that in the early years of Hitler's power "large numbers of intelligent and humane persons 'believed' that the Eastern adventure was a matter of necessity for their own survival." The situation in Japan seems to be even more clear-cut. Crowding there seemed so serious to the people that, when their attempt to conquer additional territory failed, they instituted a strong population control program.

Finally in 1969 the world saw the first war to be openly acknowledged to have population pressures as a major cause. El Salvador and Honduras fought a brief and violent conflict over frictions originating in a flux of Salvadoran migrants into Honduras. The migrants were moving from hideously overpopulated El Salvador in search of land and jobs. Since Honduras is itself overpopulated, trouble was inevitable.

There is every reason to believe that diminishing population pressures will reduce the probability of war, although it is difficult to predict how much of a reduction changing this single factor would produce. It is certainly clear that if population growth proceeds much further the probabilities of wars will be immensely increased.

Chapter 6
WHAT IF I'M WRONG?

Any scientist lives constantly with the possibility that he may be wrong. If he asks important questions, it is inevitable that some of the time he will come up with wrong answers. Many are caught before they see print; many are enshrined in the scientific literature. I've published a few myself, as some of my colleagues would gladly testify. Therefore it is important for you to consider that I, and many of the people who share my views, are just plain wrong, that we are alarmists, that technology or a miraculous change in human behavior or a totally unanticipated miracle in some other form will "save the day." Naturally, I find this highly unlikely; otherwise I would not have written this book. But the possibility must be considered.

To cover this contingency, I would like to propose an analogue to Pascal's famous wager. Pascal considered the only safe course for a man was to believe in God. If there was no God, it made no difference, but if there was, you ended up in heaven. In other words, play it safe. If I'm right, we will save the world. If I'm wrong, people will still be better fed, better housed, and happier, thanks to our efforts.

Will anything be lost if it turns out later than we can support a much larger population than seems possible today? Suppose we move to stabilize the size of the human population after the "time of famines" at two billion people, and we achieve that goal by 2150. Suppose that in 2151 someone invents a machine that will produce nutritious food or anything else man wants in limitless quantities out of nothing. Assume also that in 2151 mankind decides that the Earth is underpopulated with just two billion people. Men decide that they want more company. Fortunately, people can be produced in vast quantities by unskilled labor who enjoy their work. In about 500 years, with the proper encouragement of reproduction, the Earth could be populated to a density of about 100 individuals per square foot of surface (land and sea). That is a density that should please the loneliest person.

Remember, above all, that more than half of the world is in misery now. That alone should be enough to galvanize us into action, regardless of the exact dimensions of the future disaster now staring *Homo sapiens* in the face.

APPENDIX: LETTERS URGING ACTION

What follows are the texts of letters that have actually been sent to the addressees urging actions related to the population problem.

Letter to a Member of the Protestant Clergy

Dr. Franklin Clark Fry, President
The Lutheran Church in America
231 Madison Avenue
New York, N.Y. 10016

Dear Dr. Fry:

As a concerned member of an L.C.A. congregation, I feel compelled to draw your attention, and that of all officers of the church, to the crises developing with our exploding human population.

It is noteworthy that in A Study Book on the Manifesto, Dr. Pichaske cites several points from an address by Dr. Frank Zeidler, a political scientist. Among these are the following:

The ideological conflict between East and West has brought about...

the loss of time and energy to solve such pressing problems as the population explosion.

The destructive use of our physical and personal resources has threatened our supplies of natural resources, polluted our water and air, and pro-provided a major source for urban and rural distress.

What is even more noteworthy, and deeply tragic, is that Dr. Zeidler's address was cited only to show that modern man is in a time of change. And not to show that the church, corporately and individually, must take a stand to protect mankind from himself.

Two Sundays ago the Gospel text was the feeding of the five thousand. It would take a miracle of vastly greater proportions, continuing for years, to keep five hundred million people from starving to death in the next ten or fifteen years.

Some of them may be saved—if responsible population control measures are taken in the next few years. These would need to be measures which would reduce the worldwide (and that of each nation) birth rate to levels near or below the current death rate. Otherwise, the world food shortage (surpluses are essentially nonexistent now, as you are well aware) will be a major factor behind a catastrophic increase in the death rate. Five hundred million deaths is a reasonable guess only if the famine and pestilence finally stimulate the implementation of long-overdue measures.

Arguments purporting to show that mankind could meet the food needs of the world of, say, 1975 by increasing agricultural yield or farming the sea fail to consider current realities. Most arable land is already under intense (probably too intense) cultivation. Our environment is rapidly deteriorating, largely as a result of our crash programs to effect some short-term good, without considering long-term consequences. Further, we are not now farming the sea; we don't know what crops to grow in the sea. And even if we could determine that, we don't have the technology to farm it economically.

In view of these and many other considerations, it is imperative that the church take action. I would urge the Lutheran Church in America to begin to educate its members to several needs: the need for responsible parenthood (which is different from "planned parenthood"), the need for reduction and regulation of the birth rate, and the need for responsible programs in the worldwide activities of the church.

Sincerely,
John A. Hendrickson, Jr.

Letter from a Catholic Scientist to the Pope

His Holiness Pope Paul VI
Vatican City
Rome, Italy

Your Holiness:

I am writing to you again as a concerned Catholic scientist. For some time now the ever-present problem of population increase has occupied a great deal of my attention. Your Holiness, there are too many people in the world today, and a decline in the birth rate does not seem to be occuring. There are no agricultural techniques that we have at present or that we will have at our disposal in the near enough future to avert a predicted massive famine. Famine will lead to war, and a large-scale war will seriously, if not permanently, shatter your hopes for world peace.

It is in consideration of the above that I am deeply disturbed by the apparent attitude you have recently taken on birth control. As you well know, the views of the most competent theologians in the Church indicate that a change in the teaching of the Church with regard to birth control would be reasonable and consistent with the concept of development of doctrine that has so long been a part of our Christian tradition. Further, it is their opinion that values you believe must be maintained when considering human sexuality and marriage would not be endangered by such a change.

If there is any hope of preventing an irreparable disaster as a result of famine (in the near future), it will have to be through massive birth control programs, employing means of contraception other than periodic continence. It is for this reason I strongly urge you to reconsider the position you have taken on birth control in the encylical <u>Humanae Vitae.</u>

> Dennis R. Parnell
> Associate Professor
> City State College
> Hayward, Calif.

Letter from a Catholic Scientist to His Archbishop

Archbishop Joseph T. McGucken
441 Church Street
San Francisco, Calif. 94114

Dear Archbishop McGucken:

It has been nearly two years since I wrote you asking that you forward to Pope Paul a copy of the "Scientists' Statement on the Birth Control Encyclical." As you will recall, this statement was signed by over 2,600 scientists from the United States and Canada and strongly protested the papal position as expressed in <u>Humanae Vitae.</u> Although you refused to forward this statement, I hope that Pope Paul eventually received and read the copy I sent to him.

Since I wrote you, about two years

ago, a sad thing has happened in the world: there are about 140 million more inhabitants. At the current rate of increase, we will double the present world population of 3.6 billion in just 35 years.

There is hunger, starvation, extreme poverty, and war in the world, to say nothing of an increasingly less fit environment. It seems completely preposterous, not only to me, but to many others, including Catholic laymen, priests, monks, and nuns, to continue the position expressed in Humanae Vitae.

The facts of human population increase and all the attendant consequences are so well known and documented that no thinking person can accept the Roman Catholic position on birth control.

I very strongly urge you to examine these facts, free yourself from your past imprinting, and come out for population stabilization and the right (if not the obligation) of parents to use chemical and mechanical methods of birth control to aid in achieving responsible parenthood.

You would not lose face if you did this. You would gain much respect, you would be doing a great deal for mankind, and would be fulfilling your role as a Bishop.

With best wishes,

Sincerely,
John H. Thomas

Letter to the President of a Television Network

President:
CBS Television Network
51 West 52nd Street
New York, New York 10019

Dear Sir:

I am extremely concerned about the worldwide population crisis, and I am even more worried about our severe domestic overpopulation problem. This is probably the most urgent problem confronting mankind both now and in the future.

As a political scientist, I am acutely aware of the difficulties caused by the population explosion. Most of our national and international difficulties can be traced ultimately to the pressures of increasing population growth. There is absolutely no doubt that our rapidly growing population magnifies our already critical social problems—environmental deterioration, urban decay, interracial strife, unequal distribution of wealth, and international conflict.

However, it is reassuring that the media are beginning to give population-environment issues the coverage they must have if the public is to understand the magnitude of the problem. I am especially pleased to see an entertaining and effective series, such as "Arthur Godfrey's America"—particularly the January 16, 1971, program on the Everglades. The discussion of the Chamber of Com-

merce's medieval attitude toward growth-
manship and the frank description of
"alligator gigging" were excellent. Mr.
Godfrey's frequent references to "food
chains" and "simplicity of life" were
accurate and effective. The program
would have been even better if you had
emphasized the negative impact of five
million additional people on the East
Coast of Florida.

Now that the media have begun to
familiarize the public with the population problem, I hope that you will increase the time devoted to this issue.
Spot commercials, discouraging large
families in your advertising and situation comedies, and frequent editorial
comments would be the most helpful in the
near future. Thank you for such encouraging efforts as "Arthur Godfrey's
America."

Sincerely yours,
Richard L. Harriman

Letter to a Senator

The Honorable George Murphy
United States Senate
Washington, D.C.

Dear Sir:

I am writing to you as a citizen who
has been increasingly concerned about
the grave problems facing our nation and
the world, many of which are due to or
at least aggravated by the "population

explosion." The situation, which is apparently approaching a crisis condition in terms of worldwide food supplies, is a primary problem for the United States as well as the rest of the world. Indeed, if we do nothing or do no more than we are doing now, the situation is almost certainly hopeless.

There is a great deal that can and must be done on both foreign and domestic fronts. On the foreign side, besides sending food to those who need it, we must vastly increase our aid to improve food production locally in underdeveloped countries. Such aid must be tied to strong population control programs. Both kinds of programs are absolutely essential if underdeveloped countries are to become self-sufficient.

Domestically, there is also much to be done. Our own population growth must be stopped if we are to solve such environmental problems as various kinds of pollution, and urban congestion, and our social ills, such as poverty, unemployment, and rising crime rates—all of these traceable at least in part to overpopulation. Furthermore, we cannot hope or expect to convince the rest of the world to stop multiplying if we do not.

I strongly urge you to give serious consideration and support to any program that will encourage our population to stop growing, whether in the form of changes in the law or changes in our welfare and social programs, and I urge you to support any policies that give positive assistance to the rest of the world in stopping population growth and increasing food production.

> Very sincerely,
> Dorothy W. Decker
> (Mrs. Harry A. Decker)

Letter to a Member of the House of Representatives

The Honorable Charles S. Gubser
House of Representatives
Washington, D.C.

Dear Sir:

I am writing to you as a resident of the San Francisco Bay Area who is deeply concerned about the exploding population —both in the world in general and as illustrated by problems in the Bay Area in particular.

The ills of overpopulation are obvious in the Bay Area: increasing smog, water pollution (especially in the Bay), water shortages, and suburbia and concrete spreading across irreplaceable orchard land. All this is aside from the traffic congestion, the noise, the rising crime rates, the riots—all the usual social symptoms of the overcrowding of people.

I feel that it is time to stop encouraging new industry and new people to come to California—time to stop hailing all expansion as "progress." I strongly object to the filling of the Bay—not only because of the earthquake hazard on such manufactured land, but also because it is altering our climate for the worse and destroying a prime natural resource and recreational facility—all to make room for more people.

I believe that overpopulation is the most important issue facing the world today and that the United States as a world leader should be doing everything in her power to meet it. Starvation is a fact of life in many areas of the world right now and will be worse tomorrow. Every incident of unrest around the world can be traced at least in part to overpopulation—and as the pressures from increased population heighten, so will the unrest. Surely there is no more serious problem.

I strongly urge you to give your serious consideration and support to all efforts, domestic and foreign, that seek to establish <u>effective</u> population control.

Very sincerely,
Ann W. Duffield
(Mrs. Wendell A. Duffield)

FOOTNOTES

1. Since the mid-1960s, the doubling time has fluctuated between 35 and 37 years.
2. J. H. Fremlin, 'How Many People Can the World Support?", *New Scientist*, October 29, 1964.
3. To understand this, simply consider what would happen if we held the population constant at three billion people by exporting all the surplus people. If this were done for 37 years (the time it now takes for one doubling) we would have exported three billion people —enough to populate a twin planet of the Earth to the same density. In two doubling times (74 years) we would reach a total human population for the solar system of 12 billion people, enough to populate the Earth and three similar planets to the density found on Earth today. Since the areas of the planets and moons mentioned above are not three times that of the Earth, they can be populated to equal density in much less than two doubling times.
4. 'Interstellar Migration and the Population Problem," *Heredity* 50: 68–70, 1959.
5. I. J. Cook, *New Scientist*, September 8, 1966.
6. Ernest F. Hollings, "The Case Against Hunger," Cowles Book Co., New York, 1970.
7. This effect is dealt with in detail in P. R. Ehrlich and J. P. Holdren, "The Impact of Population Growth," *Science*, in press, 1971.
8. The birth rate is more precisely the total number of births in a country during a year, divided by the total population at the midpoint of the year, multiplied by 1,000. Suppose that there were 80 births in Lower Slobbovia during 1970, and that the population of Lower Slobbovia was 2,000 on July 1, 1970. Then the birth rate would be:

Birth rate $= \dfrac{80 \text{ (total births in L. Slobbovia in 1970)}}{2,000 \text{ (total population, July 1, 1970)}} \times 1,000$

$= .04 \times 1,000 = 40$

Similarly if there were 40 deaths in Lower Slobbovia during 1970, the death rate would be:

Death rate $= \dfrac{40 \text{ (total deaths in L. Slobbovia in 1970)}}{2,000 \text{ (total population, July 1, 1970)}} \times 1,000$

$= .02 \times 1,000 = 20$

Then the Lower Slobbovia birth rate would be 40 per thousand, and the death rate would be 20 per thousand. For every 1,000 Lower Slobbovians alive on July 1, 1970, 40 babies were born and 20 people died. Subtracting the death rate from the birth rate gives us the rate of natural increase of Lower Slobbovia for the year 1970. That is, $40 - 20 = 20$; during 1970 the population grew at a rate of 20 people per thousand per year. Dividing that rate by ten expresses the increase as a percent (the increase per hundred per year). The increase in 1970 in Lower Slobbovia was two percent. Remember that this rate of increase ignores any movement of people into and out of Lower Slobbovia.

9. McGraw-Hill Book Company, New York. 1965.
10. W. H. Freeman, San Francisco, 1970.
11. Human brain size increased from an apelike capacity of about 500 cubic centimeters (cc) in *Australopithecus* to about 1,500 cc in modern *Homo sapiens*. Among modern men small variations in brain size do not seem to be related to significant differences in the ability to use cultural information, and there is no particular reason to believe that our brain size will continue to increase. Further evolution may occur more readily in a direction of increased efficiency rather than increased size.
12. This is, of course, an oversimplified explanation. For more detail see Ehrlich and Holm, *The Process of Evolution*, McGraw-Hill Book Company, New York. 1963.
13. These data and those that follow on the decline of death rates are from Kingsley Davis's "The Amazing Decline of Mortality in Underdeveloped Areas," *The American Economic Review* 46: 305–318.
14. August 7, 1965.
15. René Dumont and Bernard Rosier, *The Hungry Future*, Frederick A. Praeger, New York, 1969.

16. *Look,* March 7, 1967.
17. W. and P. Paddock, *Famine—1975!,* Little, Brown, Boston, 1967.
18. Georg Borgstrom, *Too Many,* Macmillan, New York, 1969.
19. Professor of Pharmacology, Stanford University School of Medicine, speaking to the Palo Alto Kiwanis Club, January 25, 1968.
20. Houghton Mifflin, Boston, 1968.
21. See, for instance, Gunnar Myrdal, *The Challenge of World Poverty,* Pantheon Books, New York, 1970.
22. Address to the American Association for the Advancement of Science, December 27, 1967.
23. G. M. Woodwell, "Toxic Substances and Ecological Cycles," *Scientific American,* March 1967.
24. R. L. Rudd, *Pesticides and the Living Landscape,* Univ. of Wisconsin Press, Madison, 1964; Frank Graham, *Since Silent Spring,* Houghton Mifflin, Boston, 1970.
25. J. L. Radomski, W. B. Deichman, E. E. Clizer, and A. Rey, "Pesticide Concentrations in the Liver, Brain, and Adipose Tissues of Terminal Patients," *Food and Cosmetic Toxicology,* 1968.
26. *BioScience,* January 1968.
27. Address to the AAAS, December 27, 1967.
28. C. F. Wurster, Jr., "DDT Reduces Photosynthesis by Marine Phytoplankton," *Science* 159: 1474–1475.
29. "Lead Poisoning and the Fall of Rome," *Journal of Occupational Medicine* 7: 53–60, 1965.
30. R. C. Hariss, D. B. White, and R. B. MacFarlane, "Mercury Compounds Reduce Photosynthesis by Plankton," *Science,* November 13, 1970.
31. H. H. Iltis, P. Andrews, and O. L. Loucks, "Criteria for an Optimum Human Environment," *Bulletin of the Atomic Scientists,* January, 1970.
32. Those who claim that population growth is only a minor factor in the environmental crisis are refuted in detail in P. R. Ehrlich, and J. P. Holdren, *Science,* in press, 1971.
33. "Population Policy; Will Current Programs Succeed?", November 10, 1967.
34. "It's God's Will. Why Interfere?", *The New York Times Magazine,* January 14, 1968.
35. *New Scientist,* July 27, 1967.
36. Enke, Stephen, "Zero Population Growth—When, How, and Why," *Tempo,* General Electric Co., Santa Barbara, Calif., January, 1970.
37. *Time,* July 13, 1970.

38. P. R. Ehrlich, "A Food Glut in our Future?", Hearst Newspapers, August, 1970.

39. *Scientific American,* November 1964, p. 99.

40. John H. Ryther, "Photosynthesis and Fish Production in the Sea," *Science,* 166: 73–76, 1969.

41. Address to the Second International Conference on War and Hunger.

42. "Phytopathology in a Hungry World," *Ann. Rev. Phytopath.* 5: 375–390, 1967.

43. Dial Press, New York, 1967, p. 161.

44. "Mass Insect Control Programs: Four Case Histories," *Psyche* 68: 75–111, 1961.

45. M. Evans and Co., New York, 1966.

46. See C. Cottam, *BioScience,* July 1965, pp. 458–459, for summary and documentation.

47. Page 123.

48. Hardin, Garrett, "Abortion—Compulsory Pregnancy?", *Journal of Marriage and the Family,* 30: no. 2, 1968.

49. *Moment in the Sun,* Dial Press, New York, p. 3.

50. *Commercial and Financial Chronicle,* August 11, 1966.

51. Quoted by LaMonte Cole, loc. cit.

52. *Scientist and Citizen,* November-December 1967.

53. *The Great Frontier,* Houghton Mifflin, Boston, 1952.

54. Vol. 155, March 10, 1967.

55. Dr. Hendrickson received an extremely favorable reply to his letter. The Board of Social Ministry of the Lutheran Church in America has a highly enlightened policy on population. It is unfortunate that this church's stand is not more widely known.

BIBLIOGRAPHY

I am listing below a series of books of general interest on the population-food-environment situation. The bibliographies in Ehrlich and Ehrlich, *Population, Resources, Environment: Issues in Human Ecology* will provide access to the technical literature for those who wish to pursue a subject in depth. A subscription to *Population Bulletin* is a "must" for all interested in the population problem. This group also publishes an annual Population Data Sheet, an indispensable source of basic information on the population situation.

Borgstrom, Georg. 1967. *The Hungry Planet*. Collier Books, New York; Collier-Macmillan, London.

Borgstrom, Georg. 1969. *Too Many: The Biological Limitations of Our Earth*. Macmillan. New York.

Brown, Lester. 1970. *Seeds of Change: The Green Revolution and Development in the 1970's*. Praeger, New York.

Carson, Rachel. 1962. *Silent Spring*. Houghton Mifflin, Boston.

Ehrlich, Paul R., and Anne H. Ehrlich. 1970. *Population, Resources, Environment: Issues in Human Ecology*. W. H. Freeman, San Francisco.

Ehrlich, Paul R., and Richard L. Harriman. 1971. *How to Be a Survivor: A Plan to Save Spaceship Earth.* Ballantine Books, New York.

Ehrlich, Paul R., and John P. Holdren. 1971. *Global Ecology: Readings Toward a Rational Strategy for Man.* Harcourt Brace Jovanovich, New York.

Ehrlich, Paul R., and Richard W. Holm. 1963. *The Process of Evolution.* McGraw-Hill Book Company, New York.

Graham, Frank. 1966. *Disaster by Default: Politics and Water Pollution.* M. Evans, New York.

Graham, Frank. 1970. *Since Silent Spring.* Houghton Mifflin, Boston.

Hardin, Garrett (ed.) 1969. *Population, Evolution and Birth Control.* W. H. Freeman, San Francisco and London.

Hardin, Garrett. 1970. *Birth Control.* Pegasus, New York.

Hopcraft, Arthur. 1968. *Born to Hunger.* Houghton Mifflin, Boston.

Lader, Lawrence. 1966. *Abortion.* Beacon Press, Boston.

Loraine, John A. 1970. *Sex and the Population Crisis.* Heinemann, London.

Loraine, John A., and E. Trevor Bell. 1968. *Fertility and Contraception in the Human Female.* E. & S. Livingstone, Edinburgh and London.

Lowe, David. 1966. *Abortion and the Law.* Pocket Books, New York.

Marx, Wesley. 1967. *The Frail Ocean.* Ballantine Books, New York.

Myrdal, Gunnar. 1970. *The Challenge of World Poverty: A World Anti-Poverty Program in Outline.* Pantheon, New York.

Paddock, William, and Paul Paddock. 1964. *Hungry Nations.* Little, Brown, Boston and Toronto.

Paddock, William, and Paul Paddock. 1967. *Famine— 1975?* Little, Brown, Boston and Toronto.

Population Bulletin. Population Reference Bureau, Inc. 1755 Massachusetts Avenue, N.W., Washington, D.C. 20036.

Rienow, Robert, and Leona Train Rienow. 1967. *Moments in the Sun.* Dial Press, New York.

Rudd, Robert L. 1966. *Pesticides and the Living Landscape.* University of Wisconsin Press, Madison, Milwaukee and London.

Sax, Karl. 1955, 1960. *Standing Room Only, The World's Exploding Population.* Beacon Press, Boston.

Shepard, Paul, and Daniel McKinley, 1969. *The Subversive Science; Essays Toward an Ecology of Man.* Houghton Mifflin, Boston.

Thompson, Warren S., and David T. Lewis. 1965. *Population Problems.* 5th ed. McGraw-Hill Book Company, New York.

ACKNOWLEDGMENTS

First and foremost I am indebted to my colleagues in the Population Biology Group, Department of Biological Sciences, Stanford University. They have spent many hours discussing the population problem with me and have made many helpful suggestions. The following have taken the time to read and comment upon the entire manuscript: David M. Bell, Peter F. Brussard, Valerie C. Chase, Lawrence E. Gilbert, Jr., John A. Hendrickson, Jr., Richard W. Holm, Andrew R. Moldenke, Dennis R. Parnell, Peter H. Raven, Margaret A. Sharp, Michael C. Singer, and John H. Thomas. I have been associated with Professors Holm, Raven, and Thomas in work on the "population explosion" for many years. Much of their thinking is incorporated in this book—I have shamelessly pirated their ideas without crediting them individually. In spite of this they have been kind enough to endorse the ideas expressed.

Professor Donald Kennedy, Executive Head of the Department of Biological Sciences at Stanford, has also read the manuscript, wielded his fine editorial pen over it, and expressed his endorsement of its contents. Professor Jonathan L. Freedman of Stanford's Department of Psychology has also reviewed the manuscript and has been especially helpful in discussing problems of crowding. Other colleagues have read the manuscript or helped me in other ways. In Stanford's Medical School these include Dr. John W. Farquhar (Department of Medicine), Dr. H. Russel Hulett (Department of Genetics), Dr. Sumner M. Kalman (Department of Pharmacology), and Dr. Sidney Liebes, Jr. (Department of Genetics). Professor Loy Bilderback of the Department of History, Fresno State College, Professor Kenneth E. F. Watt of the Department of Zoology, University of California at Davis, and Professor Joseph H. Camin of the Department of Entomology, University of Kansas, in addition to reading the manuscript, have discussed problems related to the book with me in great detail. Many of their ideas have been included. Many colleagues at other institutions have encouraged me both in person and by mail, and the fact that I cannot list them does not indicate a lack of appreciation. My intellectual debt to the many writers on this subject who have preceded me should be obvious from the references and bibliography.

My attorney, Johnson C. Montgomery, has had a long-term interest in the causes and cures of the population explosion, and we have spent a great deal of time together conferring on various aspects of the problem. He and his wife, Nancy Riva Montgomery, have both read the manuscript critically. Their assistance and ideas have been invaluable. I am also grateful to Mrs. Harry A. Decker, Mrs. Wendell A. Duffield, Mrs. Lawson Bavelas, Mrs. Michael Singer, Mrs. Peter Duignan, and Mrs. Lawrence E. Gilbert, Jr., for their aid in preparing the manuscript and for their suggestions for its improvement.

My wife, Anne, has been my constant collaborator in my work on the population problem and is virtually a co-author of this book. My mother, Mrs. William Ehrlich, is an English teacher. She also read and criticized the manuscript. She wishes it publicly stated that she is not responsible for my abuse of the English language. She agrees heartily with what I say in the book. Recently she told me, in the middle of an argument about why I had not taken Latin in high school, that her only regret is that she found out about birth control too late (the meaning of that statement is obscure to me, but she insisted that I include it).

UPDATE—1978

A decade has now gone by since the first edition of *The Population Bomb* was written; seven years since it was revised. A great deal has happened since 1971, but a great deal has remained the same. First, and most important, the human population is still growing at close to 2% per year. This means a doubling time of between 32 and 40 years, depending on whether the actual rate is 1.8%, 2.2%, or somewhere in between. Most sources put it at 1.8 or 1.9% for the mid-1970s.* I would like to believe them, because it means there has been some slowing down.

Where there certainly has been a slowdown is in the overdeveloped countries, including the United States. In the U.S., one of the most encouraging things that could happen did happen: since 1971 the birthrate has dropped precipitously, actually descending below "replacement reproduction." This means that each couple is now having, on the average, slightly fewer children than would be necessary to replace them in the next generation.

The decline of the U.S. birthrate is certainly the most cheering event on the population-resource-environment front in the last decade. Population growth in the

* Unless separately footnoted, documentation for facts in this Update can be found in Ehrlich, Ehrlich, and Holdren, *Ecoscience*, W. H. Freeman and Co., San Francisco, 1977.

United States is the most serious in the world because of the extremely high impact that Americans have on the environment. Per capita energy consumption is perhaps the best available measure of the level of assault that a nation places on the essential life-support systems of the planet. By those standards, for example, the birth of an average American baby is about twice the disaster for Earth as the birth of an average English baby, and some 57 times the disaster of the birth of an average Indian baby! So a reduction in the birthrate of the United States means an increase in the chances that the ecological systems which support all of our lives will be able to continue to do so in a satisfactory manner.

When the first edition of *The Population Bomb* was written, demographers thought it would take many decades for family sizes in the United States to decline to replacement level. In fact, because the women born during the post–World War II baby boom were coming into their peak reproductive years, it was thought that the crude birthrate (number of babies being born divided by the number of people in the population) would go up rapidly in the early 1970s. The demographers' reasoning was impeccable—the higher the proportion of women of reproductive age there are in the population, the higher the birthrate is likely to be. They were dead wrong. No one anticipated the rapid change of reproductive behavior that occurred in the early 1970s. Young couples had so few babies that, even though there were many more young couples than a few years earlier, the overall birthrate came down.

The causes of this dramatic decline are not entirely understood. Certainly, economic factors—in particular a shortage of jobs and a generally dim economic outlook—played a part. And surely the women's liberation movement also played a role—many young women saw an opportunity to do something with their lives besides simply stay home and raise children. This is an excellent example of a progressive social movement, one bringing greater equity to the women in our population, and having an extremely desirable side effect. Of course, heightened awareness of the population problem seems also to have played a role in reducing birthrates. People became concerned not just about the *number* of the children that they could or should have, but also about the *quality* of the lives those children were likely to be able to lead. The Zero Population Growth (ZPG) movement undoubtedly played a role here, and some feel that *The Population Bomb* may have too.

Unfortunately, publicity about low U.S. birthrates has led many people to believe that we have achieved zero population growth. This is not the case. Because generations live side by side—grandparents with grandchildren—population growth will continue for 40 or 50 years even at the present low fertility rate. This is because there is such a huge proportion of young people, born during the baby boom of 1947–1967, who are today's and tomorrow's parents. In contrast, there are relatively few old people who contribute to the death rate. But, as the proportions of the different age classes shift towards more and more people in the older age classes, the U.S. population will stop growing around the year 2025, with a peak population of about 250 million (assuming completed family sizes and legal migration rates do not change significantly and there is no illegal immigration). After that, a slow decline will take place.

Not that this is something to be complacent about. The additional 30 million people—equivalent to the populations of the states of New York and Pennsylvania combined—would put a much greater strain on our resources and our environment than their numbers imply. Therefore, even though the population story in the U.S. in the 1970s is so largely a success story, we could stand to reduce our birth rate even further so we can reach ZPG even sooner. The National Commission on Population and the American Future concluded in 1972 that stopping growth as soon as possible was in the best interest of the nation. But the government has yet to establish an official policy—or even a position—on population growth in the U.S. And, although abortion has been legalized, the government has recently refused to provide funds for abortions for poor women —who are apt to need it most.

The population picture in the underdeveloped world is not so encouraging. A few, mostly small, UDCs have begun to see some success in their population programs. One of these is Costa Rica, which had a doubling time of 17 years in the mid-1960s, but by 1976 it had reduced its birthrate from over 40 in the 1960s to 28 and increased the doubling time to 30 years. But, even if the decline in fertility continues, the Costa Rican population will soar from 2 million in 1977 to about 5 million early in the next century. If the fertility decline doesn't continue, Costa Rica can ultimately expect 6 million or more.

This "population momentum," caused by the predominance of young people in rapidly growing populations, is the reason why UDCs can't afford any further delay in establishing population control. Costa Rica is not unique. Quite a few other countries—Taiwan, South Korea, Hong Kong, Singapore, Sri Lanka, Barbados, Trinidad, the Bahamas, Cuba, and possibly China, among others—have all reduced their birthrates to below 30. And all of them can look forward to *at least doubling* their populations in the next 75 to 100 years, unless disaster strikes and death rates rise.

China is the big question mark. Even its present population isn't known with certainty. Estimates range roughly from 825 million to 950 million for 1976. Fragmentary reports indicate that China's population control program is remarkably successful. There is no question that it is the strongest program in the world. All forms of birth control, including abortion and sterilization, are available free or at low cost to everyone through China's effective health-care system, which is being extended to even the remotest rural areas. In contrast to what has happened in other UDCs, birth control thus is being offered along with death control. Very strong social and political pressures also are exerted to limit families to a maximum of two children; young people are expected to marry late; and women are fully employed and are educated as well as men are.

China's success is showing the underdeveloped world how to do it. It now appears that building factories and encouraging urbanization is the wrong way to encourage low birthrates. Provision of health care, education (especially for women), social security, jobs, and a hope for a better life seem to be the crucial factors. In general, where these things are happening, birthrates are falling. And in countries where there has been little or no improvement in the lives of the poorest one-third to one-half of the population, there has been little or no reduction in birthrates. This is so even though death rates in UDCs have generally continued to drop, and the richest one-third of their populations may have gotten richer.

Unfortunately, the majority of UDCs are still in the latter category, including some of the largest: India, Pakistan, Bangladesh, and Indonesia. India in desperation resorted to coercion in its population program in the mid-1970s, and Indira Gandhi's government was thrown out of office largely as a result. Many of these countries, some of which are the poorest, most undernourished, and most overpopulated in the world, are prime candidates for a death-rate solution to the population explosion. If these UDCs manage to avoid mass famine or ecological collapse, and even if they succeed in bringing their fertility down to replacement levels by

2000, their built-in population momentum guarantees that they will have somewhere around *two and a half times* as many people as they did in 1970 before they stop growing. And the chances of reducing fertility that far that fast are pretty dim for many of those countries.

Most tropical Latin American countries still have very high birthrates with little or no decline in recent years; nor in many of those countries is there much sign of serious governmental commitment to the family planning programs that have been established. Africa also remains a demographic disaster area. On that disease-ridden continent, death rates still tend to be high, and in most African countries family planning programs are just getting off the ground. Therefore the prospect is for the already rapid population growth in Africa to accelerate as disease-control measures lower death rate. At least some progress in reducing birthrates has been made in many Asian countries, but some of them are among the poorest and most overpopulated nations on Earth. Even adding 50% more people to the populations of countries like India and Bangladesh could spell disaster—and the addition of many millions more than that is in the cards if famine can be averted.

Food

What about the food situation? As was predicted, food shortages have been prominent in the news of the past decade. When the weather was good for agriculture, they faded from the news; when the weather was bad (as during the Sahel drought and when overall world food production dropped in 1972 and 1974), hunger made the headlines. In each of those two years, food production dropped by 4 to 5%, while the population continued to grow by 2%. Higher food prices and depletion of reserves were the result. By the end of 1974, grain reserves were very low, and deaths from starvation subsequently rose in the poorest and hungriest nations.

Even before then, the United Nations had conservatively estimated that nearly half a billion people, mostly children under five years old and mostly in UDCs, were chronically undernourished. Millions of them die each year, and many of those who survive may suffer permanent damage as a result of early deprivation. There has been no improvement in this chronic situation since 1974; indeed, UNICEF recently estimated that as many as a billion people—one-fourth of the human population—are inadequately fed today.

The future outlook remains bleak, also. Most projections for food production indicate that, despite the Green Revolution and other efforts to increase production in UDCs, they will continue to become more, not less, dependent on food imports to feed their populations in the next few decades. Most UDCs have concentrated on urban, industrial development in recent years, neglecting the vitally important agricultural sector. And where effort is put into that sector, it all too often goes into crops like sugar cane, coffee, and jute for export rather than into food to meet the nutritional needs of local people. The foreign exchange generated by such exports frequently goes for the purchase of things like automobiles and appliances for local elites.

Where modern high-yield agricultural technology (the Green Revolution) has been introduced (primarily in Asia and Mexico), it has tended to be adopted by the larger, richer farmers who could afford the necessary inputs: fertilizer, pesticides, and irrigation water. Small, poor farmers were left out of the competition, and landless laborers were squeezed out as landowners switched to farm machinery. The landless poor have flocked to the cities, adding to the already serious unemployment problems there. An effort must be made to provide high-yield seeds plus water and fertilizer to poor subsistence farmers, and the effort should be supported by a labor-intensive rather than a machine- (and energy-) intensive technology. Otherwise the Green Revolution may turn out to be another boondoggle with limited benefit and with a high social cost. A labor-intensive system can work; China is using one with considerable success.

Whether the North American breadbasket (the U.S. and Canada—by far the largest exporters of food in the world) can continue to raise its grain production as rapidly in the next 30 years as it did in the last is a tough question. We are expected to feed our own growing population, continue shipping large quantities of grain to Europe, Japan, and sometimes the USSR, and provide rapidly increasing amounts to the poor countries.

It's not clear that we can do it. Many experts think that the scope for further increases in food production in the U.S. and other ODCs is not as great as nonagriculturists think. We've already had our Green Revolution; most of our crops are high-yielding varieties. To keep production up, American farmers are mining irreplaceable (on any useful time scale) groundwater resources in many parts of the country. The United States is also abusing soil and losing it to erosion by overintensive farming, overgrazing, and deforestation. When the Soil Bank was abolished in 1975, planted acreage was increased by 12% over the early 1970s. But 1975 production—a "bumper" year—was less than 2% higher than that of 1973, the previous record year, and average yield (production per acre) was 2% *lower* than in 1973.* The land that had been in the Soil Bank, of course, was each farmer's poorest piece, or it was between rows of crops. (When plants are grown closer together, their productivity drops because they shade one another.)

The great unknown factor that will determine success or failure in feeding the human population in the near future is the weather. Bad weather was mainly responsible for the food production reverses of 1972 and 1974 (including in the supposedly dependable U.S.). Climatologists warn us that the period 1930–1960, until recently by convention defined as the standard for "normal" weather, was actually abnormally benign. What we can expect in the future is far less predictable and stable weather and more frequent crop failures.†

* Data from the *Statistical Abstract of the United States 1976.*

† Schneider and Mesirow, *The Genesis Strategy,* Plenum, New York, 1976.

At the very least, we should be preparing for such eventualities by establishing a worldwide system of grain reserves sufficient to see us through a few bad years. Should food production drop 4 to 5% two years in a row, given present reserves, millions of people would almost certainly be starving in UDCs by the end of the second year—unless Americans and Europeans substantially reduced their meat consumption, which seems unlikely. So far there has been a lot of talk about establishing a Food Bank, but far too little action.

Energy and Other Resources

The first "energy crisis," of 1973–74, came as a huge shock to Americans, accustomed to taking resource supplies for granted. Shortages of other items cropped up at the same time, often ripple-effects of the oil shortage. But once the crisis was over, it was chalked up to politics, and complacency (as with food supplies) reigned once more. The complexities of the markets, the natural urge of resource owners to "get theirs" while the getting is good, and the hopeless ignorance of most economists and politicians as to the true nature of resource shortages have kept the public in a constant state of confusion. Insane as it may seem, years after the first energy crisis and rising energy prices began to plague the United States, the nation still has no comprehensive energy policy, and the majority of Americans do not believe there is any need to conserve! Indeed, surveys show that the public doesn't know—or refuses to believe—that we are importing nearly half of the huge amount of oil we consume. Our food exports are not an act of generosity. Without the foreign exchange they earn, we would be bankrupted by our oil-import bill.

England, a nation that imports both its oil (which it uses far more frugally than we do) and half of its food, is only hanging on until its North Sea oil wells can produce enough oil to meet domestic energy needs and earn some foreign exchange. And, when the North Sea oil is gone, what will England do for an encore?

The outcome of the current energy debate going on in scientific and government circles, but blithely ignored by most of the public, will have an enormous impact on our future way of life, and that of our children and grandchildren as well. Basically, the choice the United States faces is this:

Will we continue along the course of the recent past, consuming ever greater quantities of energy, wasting vast amounts in the process, trying to meet rising demand with costly high technologies such as nuclear power, coal gasification, and oil shales?

Or will we opt instead for what Amory Lovins calls the "soft energy path," converting as much as possible to renewable, efficient energy sources such as solar, wind, hydroelectric, tidal, with a sparing use of remaining fossil fuels to build a bridge to the new energy system?*

The first, "hard energy path" carries hidden implications for our way of life. There are serious hazards to society attached to widespread deployment of nuclear power, for instance. These include the possibility of sabotage and blackmail through stolen nuclear materials, the dangers of putting potential nuclear weapons in the hands of many nations, and the enormous problem of safeguarding growing amounts of dangerously radioactive waste material produced by nuclear plants for hundreds of thousands of years.† Protecting human society adequately from these hazards would require extremely strict security measures—in essence, a police state. Moreover, very heavy technological, resource,

* Lovins, *Soft Energy Paths*, Ballinger, Cambridge, Massachusetts, 1977.

† For a discussion of these and other problems with nuclear power, see Ehrlich and Ehrlich, *The End of Affluence*, Ballantine, New York, 1974. For more technical details, see Chapter 8 of Ehrlich, Ehrlich, and Holdren, *Ecoscience*.

and capital investments are required by this sort of energy system, depending primarily on nuclear power, strip-mined coal, oil shales, and oil and gas from increasingly remote sources. The hard energy path also necessarily means a highly centralized system of energy delivery, which tends to be both wasteful of energy and highly vulnerable to disruption on a large scale, either through accidental breakdown or deliberate sabotage. And the environmental threats, both to human health and natural ecosystems, of this path are very considerable. So are the demands on other resources to build and sustain the system.

The soft energy path, by contrast, offers none of the hazards of nuclear power. It would be relatively flexible, decentralized, and diversified, fitting the energy delivered to its end use. All this would minimize energy wastage and dependence of consumers on a centralized power grid. Breakdowns would inconvenience relatively few people and might often be repairable by the consumers themselves. There would be no need for police-state security measures, for a decentralized system would be comparatively invulnerable to sabotage, and the technologies could not easily be converted to destructive weapons.

Any energy system used by society will have an environmental impact, but simply by being much more efficient in its energy use alone, the soft path would have a reduced impact. Any energy system also is bound to make resource demands, but efficiency would tend to reduce these too. In both cases, there would be qualitative differences in the impacts as well. Contrary to the propaganda put out by nuclear power boosters, the soft energy path would be much more of a boon to employment than would the hard path. Hard energy technologies require a small army of nuclear engineers, coal miners, oil-rig operators, and other, mainly highly trained, technologists, often working under hazardous conditions. Soft energy technologies, in contrast, would require a *large* army of carpenters, plumbers, metal workers, makers of small machinery, tinkerers, and engineers.

Should the United States choose the soft energy path, the betting is that other ODCs, which are more or less dependent on American technology to carry on their nuclear and other high-technology programs, would follow suit. Inevitably, so would UDCs, for which high-technology energy systems are poorly suited besides, and for most of which the availability of sufficient capital and materials to bring their energy consumption up to ODC levels is lacking.

It should be borne in mind that the greatest danger represented by the energy crisis is that of *too much energy use* by humanity, not insufficient supplies. Environmental constraints, whether by the effect on worldwide climate of unavoidable heat releases from energy use, or by environmental destruction caused by the effort to obtain ever more resources, both fossil fuels and other materials, will at some point bring the growth in energy use to a halt. Today there is little public recognition in the U.S. or elsewhere that such limits to growth in energy use exist. Even less is it understood that resource constraints may make it impossible to change our minds later if we embark on the wrong energy path (by choice or by default) in the next decade.

Constraints to growth are beginning to make themselves felt in many areas besides energy. Many of Earth's nonrenewable resources are being depleted at unconscionable rates (although careful recycling could alleviate some of this problem). And many renewable resources (such as fish stocks, whales, redwood trees, groundwater, etc.) are being exploited at rates that promise to convert them rather soon into nonrenewable resources. As amounts of remaining exploitable resources dwindle, and the number of people increases, the *per capita* availability of resources shrinks even more rapidly. Limits to growth in resource consumption are visible now, but hardly anyone seems to have noticed.

The Environment

There has been some progress in attacking the more obvious symptoms of environmental deterioration in the overdeveloped countries, such as air and water pollution. One can certainly be cheered by the increased awareness of environmental problems in the general public, especially in the United States. In the decade since *The Population Bomb* was written, environmental issues have become major concerns, and social decision-making increasingly is taking these concerns into account.

Many of the more insidiously dangerous pesticides, including DDT, have been banned or at least severely restricted in their use. Phosphates have been reduced or eliminated from detergents. The environmental hazards to be found in factories from chemicals or other dangerous materials such as asbestos are increasingly being scrutinized and subjected to regulations to protect workers (and consumers too). A great deal of attention has been paid to assaults on our bodies by pollutants that tend to shorten our life span and make our lives less agreeable as we live them. It is now recognized, for instance, that at least 80% of cancers in the U.S. (and presumably other ODCs) have environmental origins. Cancer can be caused by all sorts of things we encounter in our daily lives, from cigarette smoke, air pollution, artificial sweeteners, hair dyes, food additives, and fire retardants, to name a few that have been discovered. Small wonder the U.S. cancer rate has been soaring!

But, even with this growth of environmental awareness, most of the attention has been focused on human health aspects, which are only part of the story. The fundamental nature of the assaults that human beings and their ever-expanding economy place on the crucial life-support functions of ecological systems remains largely unrecognized. One should always keep in mind these free public services that natural systems perform: maintaining the quality of the atmosphere (including the ozone shield), recycling all of our wastes, operating the hydrologic and nutrient cycles, controlling the overwhelming majority of potential crop pests and disease vectors, generating and maintaining soil fertility, and providing food from the sea. If these systems broke down and no longer provided these services, in most cases we would not even know how to replace them. Where we do know how, it would clearly be impossible on the scale required. Yet every time a field is put to the plow, a forest cleared, a piece of land placed under concrete, or a novel chemical released into the environment, the systems are further damaged.

While humanity can do certain things to soften its assault on these life-supporting ecosystems, a very fundamental physical law—the second law of thermodynamics —makes it clear that there are severe restrictions on how much the blows can be softened. Either expanding population size or increasing affluence in a stationary population would inevitably lead sooner or later to a breakdown of these systems; when both the affluence per person and the number of people are increasing simultaneously, the fundamental limits can be approached with astonishing speed. Nothing could be clearer from the most elementary understanding of ecological principles and what might be called an iron law of growth: *on a finite planet neither population size nor the level of economic activity can continue to increase forever.*

A Look Back at the Scenarios

Events since 1971 have, as expected, made the scenarios of even the revised edition of *The Population Bomb* largely obsolete. This was inevitable; scenarios are stories about the future designed to help people think about it. They are *never* predictions. It is interesting and perhaps instructive, nevertheless, to examine them in retrospect. We can count ourselves lucky that nothing resembling the first two scenarios has occurred, although in either case the general pattern of events still cannot be ruled out for future decades.

The first scenario, based on climate-induced worldwide famine leading to war, is no less likely to occur in the next 10 to 20 years than it seemed in 1971. The second scenario, postulating a worldwide epidemic that decimates the human population, is also by no means impossible, although Lassa Fever is unlikely to be the responsible agent. Lassa Fever, it has been discovered, loses its virulence as it is passed between human beings, and an effective vaccine has been developed against it. But who can say that no other lethal new disease will ever emerge as suddenly as Lassa Fever did in 1970, against which human beings have almost no resistance?

The third, "favorable" scenario is especially interesting. Some of the events and trends it discusses have indeed happened: the end of the war in Indochina; the opening of trade with China and Cuba; increasing frequency of local famines; declines in fish catches; commodity supply shortages in ODCs; pressure to change ODC–UDC trade practices to be less exploitive of UDCs; new attention to agricultural development in UDCs on the part of foreign aid agencies.

On the other hand, some of the other needed changes described have not materialized, or, at best, progress toward them has been glacially slow. Among these are the firm establishment of a world food reserve, establishment of anything like an International Survival Tax or other form of wealth transfer on a significant scale, and serious reform of the world trade system. The United States has so far made little effort toward conservation of material and energy resources, including large-scale recycling of minerals. "Spaceman morality" remains almost a lunatic-fringe ideology, seriously practiced only by some environmentalists in a few ODCs. The general prospects for the world have not changed much; merely by changing a few dates, this scenario's credibility could be restored.

What Is the Outlook?

There is, nevertheless, some hope that the needed changes can yet be instituted. What has been so immensely cheering to me about the decline in American birthrates, for instance, is not so much easing of pressures on the American and global environment as a clear sign that large-scale social changes can occur very rapidly. I thought, along with virtually all other observers of the social scene, that many decades of effort would be required to bring American reproduction to the replacement level. And like the others I was dead wrong. At least in a society with a high literacy rate and good communications, it's clear that when the time is right, social change can be blindingly swift. If civilization is to get through the crucial decades ahead, many other swift social changes will be required. So the experience with the American birthrate is a great cause for optimism.

Today the task of converting the U.S. and other ODCs from a growthmanic economy to a steady-state economy seems at least as difficult as the task of rapidly lowering birthrates seemed a decade ago. It's not that it could not be done rapidly if we wished to do it, but the social will does not seem to be present. Yet now it is not altogether unreasonable to hope that when the time is right, it might all come together at once. The absurd notion that the benefits of economic growth in ODCs still outweigh costs might disappear as rapidly as the absurd notion that large families are better than small ones did.

Thus, in 1978 one can be a bit more optimistic about what *might* be done than one could in 1968. On the pessimistic side, however, the worldwide population-resource-environment situation deteriorated dramatically over the last decade, and corrective actions taken thus far have amounted to little more than giving aspirin to a cancer patient. The problems loom larger as time grows shorter.

Of course the outlook for humanity depends on solving problems in addition to those of numbers of people, the aggregate level of their economic activity, and the aggregate level of their impact on the vital ecological systems that support society. As noted above, different nations and groups within nations make very different contributions to the assault on Earth's ecological systems, and of course different nations and groups get very different benefits in return for those costs that are exacted upon the ecosystems.*

One of the most obvious characteristics of *Homo sapiens* in the late 1970s is a serious maldistribution of just about everything. Goods, including food and various services, are distributed unequally among continents, among nations within continents, among areas within nations, among families within areas, and even among people within families. Tragically, for example, in the hungriest families children often get less than their "fair" share of the family's food, even though it is

---

* The idea that blacks make a disproportionate contribution to population problems in the United States is 180 degrees from the truth. So is the notion that population control is a genocidal plot against blacks, but the idea is given credence by the racism of some advocates of population control. This latter issue is explored in detail in Ehrlich and Feldman, *The Race Bomb*, Quadrangle/The New York Times Book Co., New York, 1977, pp. 37–44.

probably accurate to say that if all the food produced in the world today were in some sense equally distributed, then everyone would have an adequate diet.

Does this mean that those who claim that there is no population problem, only a problem of distribution, are correct? Absolutely not. Population pressures are a product of animals *as they exist,* not as they might be. If lions ate grass instead of antelopes, the plains of Africa could support many more of them before the plains would be overpopulated. Similarly, the carrying capacity of Earth for saints is considerably higher than the carrying capacity for *Homo sapiens.* In theory, the problem of human overpopulation could be solved by a reduction in population size or by a change towards more saintly behavior.

The current situation of global overpopulation is so serious, and the built-in potential for further population increase is so great, that the only sensible strategy for humanity today is *to end population growth and start a population decline as rapidly as is humanely possible, simultaneously striving to achieve a more equitable distribution of the food and other goods of this planet. Limiting births and increasing social justice are not alternative strategies to preserving society, they are necessary complements.*

RECOMMENDED READING

General

Ehrlich, Paul R., Anne H. Ehrlich, and John P. Holdren. 1977. *Ecoscience: Population, Resources, Environment*. W. H. Freeman, San Francisco. Designed to provide the concerned layperson with an up-to-date overview of the human predicament. More than 1,000 pages, about 2,000 footnotes integrated with 3,000 annotated references, over 400 tables and illustrations. Available in paperback at $19.95.

Specific

Daly, H. E. 1977. *Steady-State Economics*. W. H. Freeman, San Francisco. This brilliant book integrates population control with the basic economics of a sustainable society. Written by one of the few economists *not* involved in optimizing the arrangement of the deck chairs on the *Titanic*.

Ehrlich, Paul R., and Anne H. Ehrlich. 1974. *The End of Affluence*. Ballantine Books, New York. Discusses various issues related to the population-resource-environment crisis, with suggestions for how the individual can improve his or her future prospects.

Ehrlich, P. R., and S. S. Feldman. 1977. *The Race Bomb: Skin Color, Prejudice and Intelligence*. Quadrangle/The New York Times Book Co., New York. Deals with the myths about race and the issue that population control is inherently racist. To be published in a Ballantine paperback edition in the fall of 1978.

Katchadourian, H. A., and D. T. Lunde. 1975. *Fundamentals of Human Sexuality*. 2nd ed. Holt, Rinehart & Winston, New York. *The* source on sex education—every American should be given this book at puberty.

Lovins, Amory. 1977. *Soft Energy Paths: Toward a Durable Peace*. Ballinger, Cambridge, Mass. The single most influential book on energy options—a subject intimately interwoven with the question of how many people the U.S. or the world can support.

Meadows, D. H., D. L. Meadows, J. Randers, and W. W. Behrens III. 1972. *The Limits to Growth*. Universe Books, Washington, D.C. The famous computer study of the Club of Rome, showing that control of *all* factors—population, economic growth, and environmental deterioration—is necessary to avoid catastrophe sometime in the future.

Schneider, S. H. and L. E. Mesirow. 1976. *The Genesis Strategy*. Plenum, New York. Excellent popular discussion of how climate changes may influence humanity's attempts to support a growing population, by one of the world's best climatologists. Available in paperback.